20 YEARS OF...

MEAN SCARY MARY

ENTERTAINING TALES of STUDENTS AND THEIR ~~SECURITY GUARD~~

by

Mary Benear

This book is an original publication. All rights reserved. No part of this book may be reproduced, distributed, or transmitted in any form or by any means, including photocopying, recording, or other electronic or mechanical methods without the prior written permission of the publisher, except in the case of brief quotations embodied in critical reviews and certain other noncommercial uses permitted by copyright law. For permission requests, write to the publisher at marybenear@gmail.com.

Copyright © 2023 by Mary Benear.

ISBN: 979-8-218-17290-9 Paperback

Printed in the United States of America.

Library of Congress Control Number: 2023904975

Any errors in references to events, historical events, places, people, and names are unintentional.

Cover designs by Ricardo Reis
Book interior design and editing by Janet Weber
Typing by Rachel Salmon
Front cover photo from 2008 senior class float photographer
Back cover photo by Janet Weber

First printing edition 2023

Publisher - Mary Benear
Howell, MI 48855
marybenear@gmail.com

Dedicated to all the students who were
the reason I had job security
for 20 years.

Howell High Forever!!

Mean Scary

Mary

2023

Preface

Have you ever wondered what situations high school security staff encounter on a daily basis? Some of it is quite unbelievable, some of it will make you laugh, and some of it could make you cry…you might never imagine the tight squeezes, antics, and serious spots that students and other people can get into in a school setting or at a school event.

Every staff person in high school security has rules set by the district that they need to follow, but each person has their own way of enforcing those rules when it comes to handling security situations with students, parents, or guests to the school complex. I'm sure over the years some of the kids didn't like me and that's okay. There were some kids over the years I didn't like either.

Chapter One

The Beginning of 'Mean Scary Mary'

I had already been working for the Howell High School Athletic Department scheduling event staff for a few years when I was approached about a new job. That year there were no female gym teachers, so they needed a woman to supervise the girls' locker room. It was part of my new job to let the girls into the locker room before gym class then lock it down while they went to class. After their belongings were secured and no girls were left behind, I would head over to the main building. I then walked the halls of the high school making sure students went to class and things were going as normally as possible. With class size varying year to year from 500 to 700 students per grade there was usually a lot of commotion. I would head back over to the fieldhouse to let the girls back into the locker room. I repeated doing this every hour.

The district had been using a contracted security team at the high school at that time which consisted of some college age kids. They could have blended in easily except that their uniform made them stand out. It was hard for some of them to enforce even basic rules because of the small age difference. At the end of the school year, district administration had decided to hire 'in house' security staff. I was hired, along with some other people, to become part of the new security team.

When you're a teenager and someone stops you from doing what you want – to them you are considered to be mean. I tried not to let the students get away with skipping, smoking, or whatever it was they wanted to do that was against school policy so I was considered by them to be 'mean.' I did not fall for their stories, and they could not sweet-talk me into looking the other way, "You're mean," they would say.

After a few years there were a lot of 'Mean Mary' stories going around campus. Middle-school kids would hear the stories from siblings or friends and seemed to believe everything they had heard. Some of the stories were true but a few became embellished a lot by the time they were retold again and again. When staff members or students would tell me the stories they heard I would shake my head and laugh, really? No one seemed to believe me, especially not the students, when I tried to explain what actually happened in some of the often repeated enhanced situations. After a few attempts to correct those inaccurate versions, I decided to just let the stories live. Years went by, and I then turned into that security guard that works at the high school – 'Scary Mary.'

Chapter Two

The Early Years

In my early years of working security every day at Howell high school I learned a lot.

You Can't Take Students Home…

Listening to some of the stories from the students was hard for me. Some kids were living with grandparents or aunts and uncles and had little to no parent involvement. They were happy for the love of family members, but felt cheated in most cases because they did not have their parents living in the same household with them. I could not imagine being that age and having to deal with some of the extra issues the kids were forced to live with outside their school environment. I was fortunate to be raised by both of my parents who were married 38 years before my Dad passed. Some stories made me want to take a few students home with me to give them the parenting they did not seem to be receiving,

I Could Not Carry Money On Me…

I was constantly lending money out. Word traveled fast around some groups of students that I would lend money out easily. At first, I went through a lot of cash giving it to students who said they needed to buy something for lunch. It took me awhile to catch on that they always promised to pay me back, but did not end up paying me back. I was lucky if two out of ten students returned the money. I felt a lot better when I found out the kitchen staff could provide lunch free if really needed. If I had money on me, I would lend it out, so I quit carrying money except for Senior Survivor Week or to pay for some fundraiser stuff I would buy.

Looks Can't Kill…

I would bust a student and the looks I would receive would be nasty enough to pierce right through me, especially if it was a drug bust or something else serious enough that the law had to become involved. If I busted their student doing something major and they had to come into school, then I was given that 'who do you think you are' stare by their parents. In later years my skin became tougher. I knew it wasn't my fault. I was just doing my job!

Not Everyone Likes the Person Behind the Job Title…

Most students were great; they would follow the rules so having us there as a security team never bothered them. Other students did not care about people whose job it was to keep them following school district rules and keep them in line. Some students would try to be really friendly with you in the hopes of getting a break when they needed it. When the break didn't come, the friendliness would stop.

Most staff persons at the high school were awesome and seemed to be happy that we had a security team on campus. However, there was one particular staff person that made it difficult for me to do my job. Not everyone is going to like you; I learned that years ago, but when you are doing your job the staff should respect you and the job you have to do. This particular teacher would constantly send kids out of his room without a pass and would cover for them if they were caught. We would continually be sending them back to get a pass and were told by the students that their teacher just said go. I don't know how he ever taught a subject if he kept getting interrupted by returning students. At one point, he actually confronted me and told me not to bother his students, he said, "They are good kids. If they are out of my classroom, they have a reason."

"First of all," I explained, "If they have a pass to be in the halls, we look at them and send them on. We check everyone in the halls. It does not matter what class they came from (like we could tell), or if they're good kids." I never understood why everyone wanted to tell me they were good kids. I know, I know, I know, but good kids can do dumb things! To this day, I still don't know how to look at a student and determine whether they are out of a classroom for a legitimate reason or not, hence the pass.

Money – Easy Come, Easy Go…

One day I had walked by a vending machine that a student had just used. The change from his purchase could be heard falling down as he walked away. "Hey, don't forget your change," I said. He turned around and stated, "I don't deal with change." "What? Well, I do," I said, and I retrieved the coins. I started noticing that a lot of students must not deal with change. I would find money almost every day I walked the halls. I still hope that when they start earning their own money that change will become important to them. When its Mom's and Dad's money – it seems to be easy come, easy go.

I'm Good with Faces – Bad with Names…

Over the years I have worked at a lot of different venues where you run into a lot of different individuals: at elections, at the strawberry patch, at *bingo*, at sporting events, etc. When I started working at the schools I realized how bad I was at remembering names. I have had many coworkers who have the skill of remembering names after hearing them one time. I was pretty good at recognizing faces, but ask me to put a name with most faces – forget it.

Chapter Three

Young Love

Ahh – young love! I remember it like it was yesterday. My sophomore year I fell in love with a senior. I had seen him a couple of years earlier when he moved into the neighborhood of Oak Grove where I spent a lot of time when I was younger. At that point, swimming and softball took up my summertime hours between farm chores. He was always hunting, fishing, trapping, or working. Finally, he started coming around the gang and we started talking and hanging out. My sophomore year my locker was at the end of the class (in the Ws) and his was close to the beginning of the seniors (in the Bs). We saw each other constantly between classes. We started dating then, and forty-five years later I still call him my best friend.

I know what young love is, but WOW have times changed. If Jeff and I snuck a kiss at school, we were nervous about getting in trouble. Holding hands was comfortable at school but that was about the extent of what was allowed.

During my early security days, I was considered a rover. I never really had a set schedule where I needed to be so the students never knew where I would show up. I encountered plenty of young love over the years, especially in the parking lot. I was always careful when I approached a car with steamy windows, but a least it was a little warning of what I might find.

A 'Bloomin' Exhibition…

One bright summer day, I was given no warning. I pulled up by the softball and baseball fields, and there on the baseball pitching mound was young love in full bloom. I think they were more surprised than me, if that were possible, when I beeped my horn. I waited for them to come toward the dug-out and hoped my red face came down a shade or two. At least the mound was covered with a blanket.

A 'Rockin' Mobile…

One fall afternoon I was asked to go to the yellow lot to check out a 'rockin' van. As my co-worker and I approached the van I realized they didn't mean LOUD music when they said 'rockin'! My co-worker pointed to me and said, "You are first, you have been here longer." This was one time when seniority was not a positive. As we walked toward the vehicle, I hoped my LOUD voice would alert the love birds that I was approaching, one can only hope. I proceeded to knock on the front window a couple of times and warned them that I would be escorting them into the school building. Finally, a young man appeared in his game day jersey. He came to the front seat followed in a couple of minutes by his girlfriend. I escorted them into the administrator's office. I don't remember him playing that night under the lights. They both had avoided making eye contact with me for a few weeks.

A 'Steamy' Stall…

"Mary, can you come down to the girls' bathroom by the auto shop," came over my radio. I was on the other side of the school on the second floor. I headed down to the first floor thinking that by the time I finally got there the vapor would probably be long gone. When I arrived, I was asked to go and escort all the occupants out of the restroom. As I approached the last stall a female came out to join me. We exited the bathroom and met the administrator just outside the restroom. He gave me a puzzled look and said, "Anyone else?" I went back inside the restroom to find a male jumping off the toilet seat, interesting. Apparently, they were going at it hot and heavy in the hall and had decided to move their party to the last stall inside the ladies' room.

I had learned to expect the unexpected.

'Cubby' Love...

Some of the back halls by the auditorium upstairs and down had cubbyholes which seemed to be favorite spots for young love going strong at any given time. The fieldhouse also had some hidden spots that young lovers would use for a minute or so. I was passing in this area when, for the first time, I had an unexpected visual of a young couple in a compromising position. I felt like yelling, "Get a room." That would have been very inappropriate so I just said, "Come with me." Cubbyholes, back hallways, locker rooms, cars, dugouts, bathrooms, empty rooms, the students thought these all seemed to be great places for chance encounters or planned encounters for young love.

The more years I worked as part of the security staff team the harder it became to embarrass me, but believe me I was always being surprised.

Mary's Work Wisdom and Common Courtesies

Flushing Toilets

No one wants to go into a bathroom and see your feces or other types of dumpings. Take the extra second to flush the toilet. Please!

Chapter Four

A Bale of What?

It was late October and the fall breeze was mild and rather warm. School had been in session for around seven weeks already so some kids were getting the itch to ditch school and enjoy an adventure with their 'peeps.'

I had done a couple of sweeps through the parking lots and was surprised to see how quiet the lots seemed. One thing I have learned over the years is that things can and usually do change in an instant.

I knew we were short on security that day, so I went inside the high school to help out. Passing time between classes and lunchtime are busy times and when you are short on staff it seems like something always happens.

I had just gone inside the main building and was positioned by the main stairs when a student named 'John' came up to me and asked if we could talk. "Sure," I replied. We stepped outside one of the exit doors for a little privacy and also so that I could hear him. During passing time in the halls the sound level can be quite deafening.

'John' stated that his friend 'Joe' had a bale of marijuana in his car. My first words were, "Yeah, right," a bale of weed, no way. I grew up on a farm north of Howell with nine other siblings and I was used to baling hay, loading hay, unloading hay, and stacking hay. I had handled a lot of bales in my younger years on the farm, they can be different shapes and sizes, but are usually large and heavy.

I said, "'John,' you and 'Joe' are friends. Why would you be telling me this, you know that now I have to check it out?" 'John' responded, "I knew you would. I'm afraid 'Joe' will be harmed if he keeps going down this new path that he is choosing to go down. He's a good kid."

I proceeded to get in touch with an administrator and I met him at the main office. I explained the situation as it was told to me, and a big grin came across his face, "A bale?" "Yes, that's the word," I replied. "Go get 'Joe,' he said."

No one enjoyed when 'Mean Scary Mary' came to their classroom and asked for them by name, usually it was not good. I escorted 'Joe' to the office and then the three of us proceeded to the gravel lot by the softball and baseball fields which was not where 'Joe' was supposed to park his vehicle.

The administrator asked 'Joe,' "Is there anything in your vehicle you should not have on school grounds?" "Don't think so," 'Joe' replied. 'Joe' hesitated, but then followed a directive from the administrator and opened his car. Nothing was found inside the car (for a teenager's car it was really clean). 'Joe' was then asked to open the trunk. He complained about his car getting searched. After a few minutes of explanation on the rights the school system had for searching cars, 'Joe' reluctantly opened the trunk. He had been persuaded that it would be the easiest way. When the trunk popped open, there before our eyes was a bale of weed. I left the lot when the police officer arrived thinking that no one would ever believe me if I told a story about a bale of weed.

A few weeks later 'John' and 'Joe' were eating lunch together in the cafeteria, so everything seemed to work out with their friendship. I hope through the years that 'Joe' knows what a good FRIEND 'John' was to him. Not sure what consequences 'Joe' had been given or if he ever found out who turned him in, but I did hear that 'Joe' had never hauled another bale of weed.

Chapter Five

Courthouse Chaos

It was a beautiful day in late May with only a couple of weeks left in the school year and we were enjoying a half day of school. When I say WE I mean the entire school community. Everyone is excited when we are released early on such a great day full of sunshine and warm temperatures.

The buses had left about half empty which was normal for half days as large numbers of kids walked uptown. The center of town was only about a mile from the school complex which held Howell High School, Freshman Campus, Highlander Way Middle School, and two elementary school buildings. The parking lots also cleared out fast unless the teachers had a professional development day (PD day).

I was so looking forward to having the afternoon off to run errands and to get home early enough to fix dinner, something I didn't get the chance to do very often during the school year. Working in the

Athletic Department after my security job kept me busy at least two to three nights a week, sometimes more. My husband and son were on their own for dinner a lot, but believe me they didn't suffer. My husband Jeff is a great cook, and my son Chris prefers his cooking. Unless it is sloppy-joes, meatloaf, chili, or a few of my other specialties, Jeff's cooking is much tastier.

    My first stop was at the old courthouse downtown to get a birth certificate for our daughter Stephanie. Stephanie was playing basketball for Ferris State and for some reason they needed a birth certificate with a seal on it. It could have saved me a lot of time over the years if I had ordered ten duplicates of their birth certificates when they were born. Year after year it seemed like I had to prove our childrens' ages numerous times. There I was, once again, visiting the county clerk's office.

    I had pulled up in front of the courthouse and noticed the yard was full of KIDS! Not too unusual I guess; the courthouse was across the street from an ice cream store and located in the middle of town. While I had observed the crowd of kids, I had noticed that they were younger than the high school age students I usually encountered. I wasn't worried about getting too much grief from middle school kids. Not that I couldn't handle it, but I was off duty! Seeing kids outside of work would be like working in a donut factory, after working all day. The last thing you would want to see was another donut (notice I didn't use a chocolate factory as an example).

    I had fumbled around in my purse to find my license and some cash. As I exited my car, a few of the kids seemed to recognize my vehicle, and were pointing at me. I regularly used my car to patrol the parking lots during the school day, but I was surprised the middle school kids knew what vehicle was mine. I heard someone yell 'MARY' and all the kids started running, really? Okay, something weird was happening. I proceeded to walk up the sidewalk towards the front door, and I noticed a couple of ladies peering out the front windows. Again, this was weird. As I approached the last step to the front door, the door had flown open, really weird. I was greeted by a lady with the question, "Who are you?" "Excuse me?" was my response. "Who are you, she continued, those kids were about to get in a fight, we just called 911. When you exited your car, someone yelled 'Scary Mary' and they all started running." I replied, "My name is Mary Benear and I do security work at the high school. Sometimes the kids call me 'Scary Mary.'" The lady then offered me a job! She had said, "If you would like to come to the courthouse on the days the schools have a half-day and just be a presence on the lawn, we're hiring." "No thanks," I said smiling, and proceeded to enter the courthouse to go purchase a birth certificate. Sometimes work follows you home, but I wasn't expecting it to get me a job offer.

Chapter Six

Dare You

So many unexpected things can happen, and usually do, throughout a school year. One of the weirdest happenings that I was involved in cost me money.

I was walking around the corner of the H hallway headed toward the front office when I heard a loud bang. I noticed a male student head-butting the front office window. A surprised look came over my face because the window didn't break. I blurted out, "I bet you can't do that again without breaking the window." The young man turned around and head-butted the window again and it shattered. Glass, glass, glass was everywhere. I stood there in total disbelief. Amazingly the young man had no obvious signs of injury except a sore head.

I escorted him to the main office where the principal was coming out of his office after hearing the commotion. He waved us into his office and questioned the student about why he was head-butting the window. The student said he was furious with an administrator over a conversation that had just ended. "I took my frustration out by head-butting the window, and then Mary dared me to do it again, he stated." The look I received from my boss pierced right through me. He explained to the young man that the window would have to be paid for. "I will pay for half," I said, because I dared him. The student left the room and the door was shut behind him. "Mary really, a dare?" my boss said. "I'm sorry, I honestly didn't think he would ever try it again," I said.

That event helped me learn that sometimes it's not good to say the first thing on your mind.

Chapter Seven

Dress Code

Wow, have times changed. I have two beautiful daughters who graduated from Howell High School in 1998 and 2000. I can't honestly remember if what they wore to school was ever an issue. Either they are making clothes so much smaller now or we have become a society of anything goes.

My least favorite job, on any given day as a member of the security team, was to enforce the district's dress code. It was a no win situation, and at times we took a lot of grief when we tried to crack down on the worst dress code violators. They wanted us to stop most dress violations early in the day so a lot of students tried to avoid being detected. They would intentionally try not to be seen by security or administrators. If it was a violation, it didn't matter to me what hour I saw it, I would address it. When I tried to explain to students why I was stopping them I usually received an earful. I still hear it loud and clear even now.

Dress Code Drivel...

You're older and just don't get us.

Why do you care, just look the other way.

I've worn this all day and no one else has said anything.

Why me, did you see what so and so is wearing?

It's not that short.

Go catch the skippers and smokers, that is more important.

Quit picking on me.

Seriously, I have nothing else to wear.

It is game day and this is my uniform, etc., etc.

Enforcing the dress code is like trying to stop the skipping problem. You cannot catch them all, but we would put a dent in it almost every day. Students couldn't wear hats and hoods per the code of conduct. Then some administrators decided we would quit enforcing that rule to make it a little easier on staff. One less reason to engage with students not following the dress code multiple times a day on a daily basis which I disagree with. Call me old-fashioned, but I always thought that not wearing your hat and hood in certain places was a sign of respect. In my opinion, it needed to be taken out of the code of conduct before they had staff stop enforcing that rule. It did take some pressure off of staff when we did not have to worry about enforcing no hats or hoods until COVID hit. Try to identify someone who has done something that breaks the code of conduct with a hood or hat on and wearing a mask.

It did not matter what season it was, dress code always seemed to be a problem. One of my big questions was, "How do parents let their children out of the house dressed with cheeks showing?" I know, parents might be at work and don't see their children leave the house, but do they buy most of their clothes?

My faith was restored in some parents when I was called to the office to take a phone call. The woman on the other end identified herself, and asked if I would do her a favor, "My daughter is in choir right now, would you please go check to see what she's wearing? If it's a little black miniskirt, bring her down to the office so I can talk with her, I'll hold. "Sure," I had responded. I walked down to the choir room feeling good that this mom was trying. I'm sure she was trying to help her daughter follow the rules – her rules and ours. I called her daughter out of choir and immediately felt bad for the mom. This put a new meaning to a little black miniskirt, it wasn't covering much. I escorted her down to the office without any explanation until I handed her the phone – "It's your mom," I said. She gave me that deer in the headlight stare as she took the phone from me. "Yes, yes, yes," she answered three questions then handed me back the phone. "My mom wants me to be by the rock in ten minutes," she stated. Her mom escorted her back into the commons and said, "She would wait for her daughter to change." She extended her hand and shook mine as she thanked me for my help. When her daughter returned, mom confiscated the little black skirt. "That's not mine," her daughter stated, "I have to give it back." Her mom said, "Her mom can call me when she needs it back." Mom turned and left with the miniskirt.

I won't say anything more about the dress code except that I believe it is okay to leave a little to the imagination.

Chapter Eight

Fender Benders

During my security career I spent a lot of time in the parking lots on the grounds of the high school. Most days I would start off watching the buses so cars wouldn't drive through while the students were being unloaded. If you think that sounds unnecessary, you would be wrong. It's surprising how many people (parents and other students) are in such a hurry in the morning. Their schedule is the only one that really matters, and they don't realize that their actions might put students' safety in jeopardy.

The buses would unload and then I would head to the other lots. My car was well known to most of the student body so they could see which parking lot I had chosen to monitor. They hated it when I drove a different vehicle. I was there to monitor the kids' driving and anything else that seemed to be out of the ordinary.

Usually when security staff or an administrator was present things seemed to run a little more smoothly.

Rainy days were the worst because no one liked to park far from the doors. Students would try to get a parking space closer to the school even if it was not in their assigned lot. Everyone would get tired of waiting their turn, even at the beginning of the day, so they would go over grassy areas and through lots to avoid the long lines.

Sometimes my schedule would allow me to work at the end of the day instead of the morning hours. I would get notified over the radio whenever there was a fender bender involving our students. Most of the time both cars were being driven by students and someone wasn't paying attention. After checking to make sure everyone was okay, I would wait with the students. Once the police or an administrator arrived, I would head to another lot. I was even sent to M-59 for a few accidents just to check on the kids and help out if I could. We would get a notification from other students or bus drivers that our students were involved in a crash. I would respond and stay until the police responded, and sometimes until parents arrived to pick up a shaken teenager.

Fortunately and thankfully, I never saw any serious injuries to students even when some cars could not be driven afterwards.

I have seen fatalities. Once, as I was the first to arrive at an accident scene, I was driving my daughter from Lansing to Mason after AAU basketball, I crested over a hill and there was a head on collision in front of us. I pulled over and told my daughter to stay in the car. As I approached the car closest to us, someone else had stopped coming from the other direction. He yelled to me, "Have you called 911?" "Just getting here," I had replied. He yelled to his wife to call 911 and then headed to the car closest to him. I approached the other car and saw a devastating scene. It appeared the driver was deceased, and the back passenger was wedged into the dashboard and was obviously gone. The person in the passenger seat was moaning so I went around the car to her side and started talking to her. She kept asking how John and his mom were doing. She must have turned her head to the right when she had seen the car cross the center line because she was pinned and could not move. It was probably fortunate for her that she could not move because she was saved from the sight of seeing her loved ones. I explained to her that the ambulance was coming to help everyone, which was a little white lie, but I felt it was a necessary little white lie. I kept holding her hand and tried to keep her as calm as possible. They finally cut her out of the car and placed her in the ambulance that had arrived.

I saw her about ten months later at the courthouse where I was subpoenaed to testify. When she realized who I was she extended her hand for a handshake. She covered our hands with her free hand and just said, "Thank you." She was in a wheelchair, but stated that she was getting better and better every day.

So, whenever I responded to a fender bender it was to make sure that everyone was okay. Only one time did I have to raise my voice at the scene of an accident. I had been called and notified of a multiple car fender bender on the service drive headed towards M-59.

When I arrived, a woman was standing by the cars yelling at the students. I had no idea whose fault the accident was, but her yelling at the students was not helping the situation. I approached the woman and in a loud stern voice I stated, "This isn't helping anyone. I need you to return to your car and wait for the police." She looked at me like 'Who the heck are you?' Before she could utter another word, I stated, "I'm Mary and I work on the security team at the high school. I'll wait with the kids, and you need to wait in your car." She gave me another look then retreated to her car and waited for the police to arrive. I did not leave that fender bender until she left the scene. Later I ran into a student's mom who was in one of the cars involved in the same fender bender. Apparently, she said, a student was not paying attention to all the cars stopped and they ran into the back of the lady's car which caused her to hit the car in front of her. She was the fourth car in the chain reaction. The mom said, "Thank you for putting that lady in her place, she was really out of control. I was just getting out of my car until I saw you coming. I knew you would and could handle her."

Chapter 9

Skipping – Skipping

One of our jobs as security staff is to help students find their class. Amazingly a few weeks into a semester they would, once in a while, forget where they were supposed to be.

One way I earned the name of 'Mean Scary Mary' was by 'busting' or stopping students from skipping. When they had their minds made up that they were not going to a class and I spoiled their plans, they were mad. ☹ "You're Mean," they would say!

I would be naive to think that we, as a security team, caught all the skippers leaving school on any given day. However, there were a lot of days we put a big dent in the skipping, and I did my share.

They had plenty of reasons to skip.

Scrambling for Skipping Excuses…

Gorgeous day,

test day,

friend asked me to go,

I was hungry,

I don't like the class,

it is Friday,

we have a sub,

I had to run a mile in gym class,

it is senior skip day, and

I want to spend time with my boyfriend, etc., etc., etc.

I believe I have heard it all at this point.

Mary is Mean…

Students would complain to me when I caught them coming back onto campus after skipping. I would explain to them that I was writing them a referral for skipping and leaving campus. They would be furious with me. They would say, "Why are you just busting us? There are plenty of other kids skipping." I would explain to them that I can only bust one group at a time. "You're mean," was usually said next.

Most of the time I would give the groups of skipping students I encountered in the parking lot a chance to explain themselves. I would get a kick out of the skipping rookies when I asked the question, "Where are you coming from?" They would look at each other like 'what should we say?' Then they would blurt out different answers simultaneously. Busted! Groups that skipped more often seemed to pick one person to do all the talking. At times the stories were quite believable then other times they were laughable. When the referrals were turned in to the office, the comments would read – The student lied about their excursion. The non-talkers would complain if I wrote they lied on their referral. I never said a word. If you're driving the getaway car after a bank robbery you are still guilty.

Several Skipping Scramblers…

If they were 'regular' skippers, I would just tell them to head inside, they would be called down later by an administrator. I would rather not waste my time listening to more excuse scrambling. Others will try to talk their way out of a referral by telling me they were called out that hour. They would tell me they just forgot to sign-out as they would be texting their parents for back-up. Thank goodness most parents would not participate in the lie. <u>Some do</u>!

Whether I worked inside or out I would try to talk the students out of leaving. They needed to go to class. Students would constantly leave through side doors to avoid the security team. If we did not recognize students when we would see them exit through side doors, we would talk over the radio to see if any other team member had recognized them. In one instance, a new teacher was standing by me when I was asking for help to identify two female students leaving out a side door. "Don't bother them, he says, I know them, they're good kids." "They're all good kids," I replied, but sometimes they make a mistake or a bad choice. Come to find out that was the sixth time in three weeks they had skipped out together. They were seniors. They had to come back to finish school after the seniors last day for a week of make-up time to graduate, at that point they were very recognizable.

Some students would smile and laugh when I told them they were not very good at skipping or lying, especially when I caught them on their first attempt at skipping.

I was not very good at skipping. I skipped twice in my high school career. The first time I was a freshman and my girlfriends talked me into walking uptown. We spent the day in one of the girl's brother's apartment watching television. We went to a store and bought some junk food for lunch. We did have a man in front of us at the checkout say, "No school today, good for you." I was terrified the whole time we would be caught. We snuck back to school and rode the bus home. Totally not worth the worry and stress I felt all day long. My parents were awesome, but I didn't want to see my dad's eyes if he received that phone call from school about me skipping.

The second time was my senior year when a bunch of us left and spent the day together. I didn't seem so stressed that day, maybe because we didn't have to go back to school to catch a bus home, we had a car. Maybe I was just older and had never been in trouble during my high school career so I thought one referral wouldn't hurt. I wasn't very rebellious.

Some students are rebellious and others are not. Believe me, a lot of times when I walked up to a car, I would see objects being shoved under seats, into pockets, or thrown out windows. When they didn't see me coming, I would knock on the window and the scrambling would begin. Other students would skip and never leave campus. They would just sit in a car (not necessarily their car) for a class period that they wanted to ditch. When I approached the car, I always expected to find something more than students just listening to music. It was refreshing when they were actually just listening to music to avoid a test, even though it was a bad choice on their part.

Skipping happened on any given day for multiple reasons, but April and May always seemed to be extra busy. The weather gets nicer, the sun shines brighter, and the students are tired of school. This is especially true for seniors who come down with 'senioritis.' I knew they got excited about all of the senior happenings and their future, but attendance still counted for grades. It's not funny when they can't participate in graduation activities because they are missing credits. Sadly, it happens to some students every year.

We have a closed campus at lunchtime for reasons that probably don't make any sense to the students. If only half of the student body wanted to leave for lunch it would be chaos. There are not enough restaurants or drive-thrus close enough to campus to accommodate all of the students in a timely manner so they could make it back to class on time. The race to leave that parking lot so that they could be first in line would cause issues. It's also easier for students to return during passing time without being detected by security. Therefore, a lunch break turns into a whole hour which doesn't help with attendance issues. On one particular day it seemed like an incredible number of groups were leaving during lunch.

It was an extremely warm and sunny day for early April and the parking lots were as busy as a grocery store. Students were going in and out almost every school entrance/exit. I parked my car and started to approach group after group after group. I questioned them on why they were coming from the parking lot and heard story after story. I recorded their names on a pad of paper so I could follow up on their story later and then write a referral if needed. I had worked here for a lot of years, but was still amused and amazed when students would give me a reason for leaving and they sounded so convincing. There were not many stories or excuses I hadn't heard before at least once or twice. After our conversation they would walk away, and you could hear them snickering like they really pulled one over on 'Mean Scary Mary'. The next day they would be called down by an administrator and realized that their lie hadn't quite worked out as well as they had thought.

Surpassed Scrambling Skipping Excuse Levels…

I had been getting really tired of all the lies that were being given to me as excuses on that day – then here they came. 'Tony', 'Mike', and 'Mark' approached me from the back of the yellow lot. They were two seniors and a junior (who in his mind always thought that he should be treated as if he was a senior). I had dealt with these 'Three Amigos' plenty of times before. This time they tried to avoid me, but the back doors by the shop area were locked so they couldn't avoid passing by me. The stories they had given me over the years had been quite entertaining, but were very seldom the truth.

If there was an assembly, the 'Three Amigos' would be the first ones out of the doors headed to the yellow lot. Somehow, they always managed to get the same lunchtime together, though they rarely saw the inside of the cafeteria. I would catch them and write referrals; they would do their detentions or lunchtime in the administration office and then lay low. After a few days they would be found again headed for the lots. Occasionally they would park in the wrong lot to try and avoid being seen leaving school property. It seldom worked because the truck 'Mike' drove was very recognizable and stood out like a sore thumb.

Believe me there was no love lost going either way between the 'Three Amigos' and me. I'm sure over their high school careers I had received a few middle fingers behind my back. The 'Three Amigos' had approached me on this day, and I decided to give them a deal. I stated, "If you guys tell me exactly where you are coming from and how long you have been gone, I'll not write a referral." "Seriously?" 'Tony' questioned as he looked at 'Mike' and 'Mark' in disbelief. "I have been told so many lies and excuses today that if you guys tell me the whole truth, I will forget this conversation ever happened," I stated. 'Mike' spoke up, "We went to lunch and the restaurant was busy so instead of coming in late to fifth hour we decided to just skip the whole class. We ate, drove around for a while, and we are just getting back to school."

"Okay, I stated, get to class and just know the next time it will be a referral."

I headed to my car with a smile on my face. I'm sure the 'Three Amigos' had a great story they were going to lay on me. Now they could save that story for another day since I promised them a reprieve for that day. I returned inside the building and wrote up quite a few referrals.

The next morning one of the administrators said, "I see you had a busy day yesterday." "Yes," I replied knowing his day was going to be really busy dealing with all of the referrals from yesterday. I chuckled as I walked away. "Have a great day," I said.

Days later I got to hear another story from the 'Three Amigos,' heavy sigh. I was extremely happy when 'Tony' and 'Mike' graduated. 'Mark' still had another year. ☹

Mary's Work Wisdom and Common Courtesies

Lunchtime, Any Time Trash…

There are so many places that have trash cans available where you can dump your fast food trash, empty bottles, and ashtrays. Better yet, just take it home and dispose of it properly. Why do you have to throw it out your vehicle window when you are driving around? It's sad when you are driving down city streets, back country roads, around parking lots, or highways and have to see trash lining the roadways. You wouldn't want people throwing their trash by your homes so respect other peoples' property. NO 'FOOTPRINT' LEFT BEHIND!

Chapter Ten

Chance Encounters

Right Place at the Right Time…

Being the security team rover, especially at lunchtime, gave me lots of opportunities for chance encounters. Sometimes students take advantage of passing time or lunchtime to do mischievous things.

Sing No More…

Walking the back hall by the choir and band rooms one day at lunchtime I saw a student duck down from looking out the window in the practice rooms hallway. The hallway is between the choir and band rooms that have 6-8 practice rooms that are regularly used by students. I entered the hallway and noticed some activity in the first practice room on the right, so I opened the door. I was greeted by four young men (A quartet?) standing around the piano bench that one of the young men had quickly jumped onto. "Hi guys, what's up?" I said. "We were just working on a song," one student replied. In most situations I encountered with multiple students, there is usually one student who will do all the talking so the story stays the same. I turned my focus to another one of the students and inquired, "Hey, are you in band or choir?" I asked. "Um no, I was just here listening to the guys, he said." There goes that quartet!

Out of the corner of my eye I saw a bag of something behind the tuba case against the wall. One gentleman said that he needed to go to class as he headed toward the exit. I stepped in front of the door and stated that we would all just hold tight as I called for an administrator. When the administrator came into the room, I opened the door and was greeted with, "What do you have Mrs. Benear?" I replied, "A couple of bags behind the tuba case and one behind the piano books." After a quick search of the room a few students dropped their heads and were led out of the practice room to the office. It was very clear that there was no singing going on, instead they were separating and bagging to be distributed later.

Everyplace and anyplace in the building or on school grounds you needed to be alert for almost anything. Over the years I'm sure I missed lots of things going on, but I sure found a lot also.

Vape No More…

I walked by a computer lab and was looking through the window and noticed a young gentleman pulling what looked like a vape out of his mouth, really, in the classroom? I entered the room and asked the teacher, who was drawing on the board, if I could borrow a student. I escorted him out and down to the office. "Administrator, there is a vape in his pocket and he was using it during class time," I explained.

Smoke No More…

Outside the west end of the fieldhouse there is a little cubby-hole by the gym door exit. On this particular day, there were two girls smoking, they quickly dropped their cigarettes to the ground, still lit. They rushed to say the lit cigarettes were not theirs, they were just talking. I replied, "I was born but not yesterday." That small cubby-hole was the source of a lot of chance encounters.

As I wandered, I would always check out the hidden areas or the quieter places. Once we installed new cameras, those places shrunk big time. Not giving away any big secrets here, we have always told the kids there are cameras everywhere. Obviously, there are no cameras in locker rooms and bathrooms, so they became popular places for mischief.

Toke No More…

One day, while walking the girls' locker room, I could hear voices. Looking around, the voices finally led me to a small back room. I pushed the door open to find three girls smoking; they were not cigarettes but some small funny looking things. The laughter went away, and heads dropped.

Propped doors are a normal thing security deals with constantly. If a door is propped and you can wait long enough, you'll have an encounter that usually turns out with the best surprised students. They come back from an off-campus adventure and think that they're home clear until they pop open the door to find 'Mean Scary Mary' waiting on the other side. Surprise. Surprise. Surprise.

Chapter Eleven

The Small Stuff

Over the years it has amazed me how some parents intervene for their student over the smallest of problems. Let your students pay the consequences for the small bad decisions they make and hopefully they might not progress to bigger stuff.

'Marie' was a perfect example of too much parental intervention. When I met 'Marie,' she was in her sophomore year and loving her high school experience. She had lots of friends, and was always smiling as she walked the halls. It was early in her senior year before 'Marie' crossed my path in a way where I had to write her a referral. I had found 'Marie' and three friends headed to the parking lots one lunch hour. I stopped them and explained the lots were off limits during lunchtime and sent them back in. By the time you're a sophomore you have surely heard that during the day you cannot go to the parking lots without permission. Everyone seems to forget some of the most basic rules if it helps their agenda.

Knowing 'Marie' had already been warned, when I found her and a friend sitting in her car during lunch it was time to write her up. Another day during third hour she came back onto campus without having signed out when she left. She received another referral. A few weeks later security caught her taking three friends off campus because no one wanted to go to sixth hour. A smell in the car had turned into a search which produced some illegal contraband for her to have on school grounds.

Mom gave an excuse for everything. Lunch in the parking lot was because 'Marie' was having some conflict with some girls and needed to remove herself from the situation. Mom gave her permission to leave during third hour to run home to retrieve a project she forgot, no call and no signing out. Sixth hour she gave permission for 'Marie' to leave, and she should not be responsible for the other students' decisions ('Marie' drove them off campus). Oh, I drove her car the day before you confiscated that illegal stuff from her car so it was all mine (yeah, right).

Once referrals are written and turned in I don't usually know what students receive for a consequence. I could ask or look it up, but to me it wasn't that important. 'Marie,' however, never seemed to receive any detention or discipline for her bad decisions. I did find it very amusing that toward the end of her senior year when 'Marie' was found at school under the influence of alcohol, Dad had come to pick her up not Mom. 'Marie' graduated but could not walk with her class, but after spending two weeks making up time, she did receive her diploma. No big smile.

Six years later 'Marie' was in town visiting family when I ran into her and her big smile. I asked her how she had been doing and what she had been up to. She was pretty honest and told me her first four years out of high school were pretty tough. I found myself in a few situations that I created that were not good. I finally decided I was the only one that could get myself together. "Loving life now," she said with that familiar smile from ear to ear. She was lucky, 'Tommy' was not so lucky.

'Tommy' was another student that seemed to be a little over protected by a family member. Not sure what his home life consisted of but grandma seemed to be his rock. Don't get me wrong, everyone needs that person in their corner who always has their back. Sometimes tough love is needed from your rock to make you appreciate the stage of life you are in at the time. Decisions you make can, and usually do, affect the next stage of your life for good or bad.

'Tommy' had his life by the horns. He did what he wanted when he wanted with no regard for right or wrong. He was old enough to have senior status, but his credits showed that he was a sophomore at best. 'Tommy' was always fighting his way out of tight spots of his own making. I wasn't involved with any of 'Tommy's' exploits until the last one. I caught 'Tommy' with a friend sitting in a car enjoying the sunshine, and some weed. The police were involved, and for 'Tommy' it was strike five on his school record. He came into school with his grandma trying to plead his case.

I really do not think that he cared at the time, but grandma cared and she wanted him to graduate. The administrator called me in after 'Tommy' left to let me know he had threatened to get even with me and the administrator for getting him expelled. We were still talking when 'Tommy' reentered the office to let us know he meant the threat. He actually shoved some objects off the desk before exiting when grandma yelled, "We're leaving."

I never heard another word about 'Tommy' until four years later. His buddy told me he had ended up in jail for writing checks and cleaning out his grandma's bank account. I felt really sorry for her and for him because maybe if he had paid the consequences for some of the smaller things he did, he would have learned. Instead, he was allowed to do whatever he wanted with no, or very little, consequence. Sadly, all of that small stuff turned into some big stuff for him.

Mary's Work Wisdom and Common Courtesies

Actions, Reactions, Consequences

A child's actions could have consequences after someone reacts to them. If a child goes through life thinking they can do whatever they want, it can lead to difficult life events.

Chapter Twelve

F-Word

When I first started working on the security team at Howell High, I was much younger (twenty years younger) and pretty set in my ways. I believed things were right or wrong, not much grey area in my mind. One thing that was never in question was how much I hated the F-word.

Overused Word...

I know that I grew up a little sheltered living on a farm, but yes, I had heard the F-word before. Never heard my parents use the F-word, but over the years it was used a little more commonly. Unfortunately, now it's a common derogatory word used by our young students and a good portion of society.

When I first started, I would take every student to the office that had used the F-word with me or a teacher. I finally learned to just write the referral and let the administrator deal with them later. I'm sure some of the administrators were tired of dealing with referrals about the disrespect students showed after being caught doing something against the school system's code of conduct.

I never let the students get away with using the F-word. Some of those students thought they were being funny in front of their friends when they told me to F-off. I never thought of it as being funny. Most students never uttered the F-word. Other students used it constantly in their everyday conversations.

'Sam' was a young man who was always in the halls, and every time I asked him to go to class, I was greeted with F-off. I was just doing my job, but on certain days when I saw 'Sam,' I felt like turning around instead of raising my blood pressure. Not in me to not do my job. I would double check to see where 'Sam' was supposed to be, but I usually knew the answer before I looked it up. I could have recited his schedule better than he knew it.

 He had chosen to forget his schedule on a regular basis. As I approached 'Sam' I was hopeful that this would be the day he would just turn around and head back to S-3 without incident. Not today. "'Sam' you should be in class," I stated. "Why do you F-ing care?" he retorted. "I really want you to graduate on time so you can get on with your life. Also, you know, it is my job," I said. He rolled his eyes and walked back toward S-3. I thought I had actually made a small difference with 'Sam' that day.

A couple of weeks had gone by since I had seen 'Sam' in the usual halls during class time. I had entered the stairwell by the choir room, and there he was smoking with his buddy. Really? "Let's go guys, head to the administrators' offices," I stated. 'Sam' and his buddy had turned around and headed towards student services with the F-bombs flying the entire time. There was a teacher in a corner room who stepped out of his classroom to check on the verbal commotion. "You okay?" he asked. "Yes, thanks," I replied.

I walked 'Sam' and his friend into the office, sat them down, and then explained to the administrator what had happened. I left the room and walked by 'Sam', and I did something unprofessional, but I'm human. 'Sam' was just staring at me, so I said, "Hey just remember a grandma busted you today," and I rolled my eyes and walked away.

Overused Finger…

Believe me, over the years I've had my share of the middle finger being given to me also, mostly behind my back, but in the later years of my career right to my face. At times it became a joke between some of the security staff. How many F-bombs or middle fingers did you receive this month? It was hard to laugh because I didn't quite understand why or when people, especially students, thought flipping people off had become acceptable behavior.

When you drive down the road and someone doesn't like the way you are driving, you'll know about it. They believe their way is the right way, so usually the horn comes followed by a drive-by finger. It's so easy to give the finger to a stranger you will probably never see again.

The schools have cameras all over the grounds and someone always seems to be watching. Students still try to deny that they gave the finger to a staff member, but there is usually camera footage for proof. It is not quite so funny when it might get you some time out of school for using that finger.

Underused Brain…

One Saturday I needed to drop off some stuff to my office before we headed north for a few days. My husband Jeff was with me, and we carried everything inside that needed to be put away. I was almost done when I noticed some skateboarders right outside the doors. It's nothing to find tables, soccer goals, benches, etc. being used for jumps. I went out the doors and asked the kids to go to the skate park. "No skating around the school," I stated. Most skateboarders would say okay, pick up their boards, and head to the skate park which was right around the corner. These four decided to question the rules because they didn't like that rule. The spokesman said, "Why do you care?" I replied, "I work here and we would like you to use the skate park we built with ramps already installed." He replied, "You didn't build the skate park," as he kept skateboarding. I said, "You have no idea whether I was involved in the building of the skate park, but I will be involved in calling the police. I can report you for damaging school property." His buddies took off for the skate park and the spokesman decided to give me two middle fingers as he was leaving. "Glad your fingers work, how about using your brain, and just follow simple rules. One day you're going to flip off the wrong person," I said. I walked back into the school just as Jeff was headed out to be my backup when he saw what was happening.

"I don't know how you do it Mary, I couldn't put up with all the disrespect." "The good kids make up for the jerks," I said.

Chapter 13

The Benches

I started working in the Athletic Department in 1994. Yes, that's a long time. I am in the fieldhouse a lot of days after school, setting up for games or getting things ready for future games. There is always something to do. After school, athletes and students congregate in the fieldhouse as they await games, practices, or are just waiting for a ride home.

The noise level can be pretty loud, but you get used to it and usually there are no real issues. I've learned over the years to tolerate most things after school hours except extreme horseplay or students blatantly disrespecting the rules. Every once in a while 'Mean Scary Mary' has to make an appearance.

One main rule I try to enforce is <u>No Sitting on Top of the Benches</u>. Sounds so trivial to a lot of students but the benches were purchased for student athletes to have a place to do homework, eat off them, store bags on, etc. etc. etc. We usually have signs up that say <u>PLEASE DON'T SIT ON TOP OF THE BENCHES. USE APPROPRIATELY</u>.

…The top of the benches are not made to support a person's weight.

…When people sit on top of the benches, they have their behinds sitting where students put their lunches or snacks (ugh).

…Sitting on top of the benches means that their feet are on the area where people sit. We don't need your footprints and dirt on students' backsides.

Some students will see me coming and warn their friends, "She's gonna yell at you." You will see them jump off quickly, which tells me they know the rules. Other students get no warning as I approach them and ask them to read the sign behind them. Sorry I forgot is a common response I receive, along with some rolled eyes and some back-talk. I reply to some of them, "You need to pick better friends; they could have warned you that 'Mean Scary Mary' was coming!" Sometimes I give the bench rule violators two choices; follow the simple rules of the fieldhouse or wait outside for your rides. Coaches, teachers, and many students have heard my loud voice yelling down the hall, "We don't sit on top of the benches!"

Mary's Work Wisdom and Common Courtesies

Ticket Taker Tolerance...

For people who think ticket takers have anything to do with setting the entry fees, you are WRONG so give them a break. They are there to help run events so your child has a chance to make memories. Without them it would be almost impossible to run sporting events. Instead of yelling at them because of the prices, throwing money at them because you are frustrated, sneaking in, or just walking by them without paying because you think you are special, give them a smile, pay the entrance fee, and thank them for their assistance. Don't get me wrong, 95% of the people that walk into a gym or a set of bleachers to watch a game are awesome. They are happy to be there to support their child who is playing a sport they love with a team of friends. But if you fall into that 5% who want to yell about every little thing, remember we are always looking for help.

Chapter 14

Job Security

There are a lot of jobs that are always in demand and highly needed. Police, firemen, doctors, nurses, truck drivers, mechanics, teachers, custodians, coaches, referees, secretaries, farmers, etc., etc., AND security personnel at Howell High School.

An average class at our high school usually runs between 500-600 students, sometimes larger. With four classes; sophomores, juniors, seniors, and freshman over at the Freshman Campus building, we have around 2,000 plus kids per day. Our high school is like a small village where anything can happen and usually does.

Fights…

There were a few years we seemed to have fights on a semi-regular basis. Some years I could only recall one maybe two fights during the school day.

We would get to fights as quickly as we could, but getting through the group of kids watching wasn't easy sometimes. When we arrived, they usually stopped quickly but there were plenty of times I had to grab a collar or an arm to let them know they needed to knock it off. Funny, they did not always seem to hear my loud voice.

The year that the high school kids were at Parker for the school year, while Howell High School was being renovated, we had one of the worst girl fights on a Friday, and I wasn't working. It had been brewing for a while, but they had told me later they had picked that Friday because I wasn't working.

Cell phones…

When I started, I enforced all the rules that were on the books. The rules have changed a bit, but some rules have carried over year after year. With a few exceptions, rules have changed to meet the times. One is cell phone use. Early on, when cell phones became popular, not every student could afford them. Teachers used to take away their cell phones when they used them during class times. They would take a bathroom pass and would be sitting in the hall or bathroom talking on their phones. I would ask them to stop talking and give me their phone, they would say things like, "I'm talking to my mom." I would say, "Could I please talk to her and tell her you are skipping class and that your teacher would like you to come back?" Out of all those years, only one student had actually let me talk to their mom. Now just about everyone has a cell phone and some teachers let the students use their phones for class activities. I sympathize with the teachers when they are giving a test and have to stop their students' cell phone use.

No Hats and Hoods…

One rule I always enforced was that no hats and hoods were to be worn while you were inside the building. I guess I'm really old school, but to me it was a sign of respect not to wear a hat or hood inside. When that rule was not to be enforced anymore, I really didn't agree, but I wasn't making the decisions. Then recently when masks were required, it made it extremely hard to identify a student who did something against school rules. Mask-hood-hat is was almost impossible to recognize a student.

Rules need to be enforced if you have them on the books. No skipping, no leaving for lunch, no smoking, no drugs, no fighting, and no bullying, are easy rules to follow and enforce. Most rules, except for dress code, were easy to enforce. I'm sure the students thought it was old-fashioned when school policy comes to dress code, but wow. My co-workers and I wondered, on some days, how students in inappropriate attire were allowed out of the house. Cold weather or warm weather the clothing items some students decided to wear to school were definitely questionable.

Everyone is Different…

Most students followed the rules but like any small town there are some that don't think the rules apply to them. I had a family of three siblings all going through the high school within two years of each other. The oldest was so polite, they always greeted me with, "Good morning Mrs. Benear," or "Have a good day Mrs. Benear," or "Mrs. Benear can I help you with anything," and always with a smile. The youngest one was in my son's class and always had a smile on his face when we interacted with each other. The middle son was a challenge. Nothing big, but he was always pushing my buttons. Leaving early, parking in the wrong lot, going out to lunch, skipping, were just a few of his school policy misadventures, and he always had an excuse and an attitude when I talked to him about anything. I honestly thought he was hoping I would get tired of making him follow simple rules and I would give up. <u>I didn't</u>! He graduated and went off to college and I really hoped the best for him. I very much enjoyed his parents, and was excited that he wasn't one of my acting out students anymore. I was always happy to see the kids get their diplomas and leave to start the next stage of their lives, just some for more reasons than others.

Two years later I was invited to his younger brother's graduation party. My son and I arrived, talked to the graduate, and then proceeded to get a plate of food. I walked up to the table and there was their challenging middle son. "Hi, how are you doing," I asked. A look came over his face of disbelief, "I'm surprised you even want to talk to me. I was quite the shithead to you when I was in high school," he replied. "You were, I called you job security because if it wasn't for shitheads like you, they wouldn't need people like me," I said. We both chuckled and then I found out about his college career, and we had a very good conversation. He actually said that he wished they would have had people like me at the college level, because it would save kids' parents a lot of money. If you fail a college course because of attendance you just repay and take it again. I took my plate and went to sit by his parents. I smiled as I said, "You guys did a good job with all three of your boys."

Conversations with past graduates are so rewarding to me. I love to hear that their life is going well; careers, families, friendships, and health, so many have such great outlooks on life.

Chapter Fifteen

Smoking Pits

Every high school has places where students know they can sneak out to when they feel the need to light up a cigarette or something a little stronger. They needed a place out of sight that gave a hint of being secure. Cars were a great spot, but not everyone drove and sometimes it was easier to sneak to the 'Pit'.

The 'Hospital Pit'...

Our biggest 'Pit,' unofficially, that the students had created was between the high school and the hospital on the next street over. It is a low area of vacant land with lots of overgrown brush and small trees. Students used a path to cut across to the hospital lots on their walk home. It looked innocent to the human eye until you took a stroll down the paths. There were several paths cut through the brush that led to little protected areas for lighting up. The areas came equipped with bigger rocks, or a bigger tree branch that had been transported in, to provide a little more seating comfort for a quick smoke break. If you went through the back of these areas, there were paths to the other side of the wooded area. The ground was usually a little wet so less people would follow you. It was a longer walk but you would come out close to the sidewalks, and students could pretend they had just walked to school. It was amazing and amusing the stories I would receive when I asked, "Where are you coming from." Their response was usually, "Home, we missed the bus." "Where do you live?" I would inquire. Before they thought too much, they would blurt out their road which may have been north of Howell. I would question, "Then why are you coming from the south? Guys, I wasn't born yesterday and if you think I believe you made a detour walking through town, come on get real."

In the early years of my security life the 'Hospital Pit' was the most popular. We were given an inside tip on a Friday that there was going to be a mini convention during fourth hour in the 'Pit.' We waited for the party to get started then put our plan into action. We placed security staff and administrators on the three major exits of the 'Pit' and then entered from the main walking path. The commotion started and we could hear and see the students running all over. The administrator I was with raised his hand and gave a command, "Stop I'm an administrator," as students had tried to sneak through the brush. A little chuckle came out of my mouth as I stated, "I don't think that's going to work, but nice try." The convention was heavily attended so the placement of staff at certain locations worked to perfection. We escorted students to the offices and found some party favors still in their possession. While they were in the office, they had given us a few more names of students still hiding or that had escaped our net. We picked up the stragglers and even found the host of the party favors so it had been a good plan.

The Howell High School smoking 'Pit' even made a Grand Rapids radio station show topic. A Howell graduate was one of the DJs on air when *School Smoking Pits* became the talk of the hour. He referred to how he had spent some quality time in the 'Hospital Pit.' He said, "He really didn't know if it was worth it. Every time he came out of the 'Pit' the same security lady always seemed to catch me. I'm not very fast, but she doesn't look like she could catch me. Somehow she always did catch me. Mary Benear did her job."

I know some students bragged that they weren't caught by me in the 'Pit.' I compare it to speeders on the expressway. They can't catch us all but when they stop someone, anyone driving by can see that they were caught by the police. We are grateful that it was someone else being pulled over because it's usually expensive, but seeing someone else pulled over does usually make us slow down. Other pits became more popular when some of the underbrush was mowed down in the hospital pit.

The 'Tennis Court Pit'...

The tennis courts have a cubby hole in the trees that provide a very good view to any incoming adults. When I saw activity, I would come out of the backside of the pool and was usually undetected. Their surprised looks were great as they tried pitching their stash in the woods – too late. Then they moved behind the next set of brush which actually had much better camouflage. I made a lot of long trips around the back side to come up behind them. The problem was that you never knew what you were going to encounter.

The 'New Pit'...

The first time I walked into the newest smoking pit, I couldn't believe what I was seeing. We found one of our lunchtime tables from the courtyard, chairs, and a couple of school desks. If they could carry and easily remove something to sit on from its intended location it could be found in the 'New Pit.' That pit could not be seen from the High School or Freshman Campus. Students had been walking back and forth between the buildings when someone noticed a detour some of the kids were making. The students that were found using this pit had to help with the closure of their space by disassembling the contents and restoring them to their proper places.

Unfortunately, since vapes have become popular, students are getting more brazen. We have even had some students caught vaping inside a classroom during class. Times are definitely changing.

Chapter Sixteen

Stalking, Really?

I know over the years I have written the same student up multiple times. It happens, but stalking, <u>come on</u>. I have explained to some parents who have accused me of stalking or picking on their child that it's just a coincidence that I keep catching their student. First of all, I have never walked into a classroom and written a referral on their student for being in class. Secondly, it is my job to try to keep students in school so that they can learn, not roam the high school grounds where academic learning is not happening. Most parents, not the student, soon realized they were just looking for someone to blame when their child did something against school policies. Parents would sometimes apologize when they realized how they sounded. Stalking is a strong word to throw around. Years later, certain parents, still think it was my fault that their kids had to serve detention – wow!

I had watched the buses unload one dark morning and noticed two students walking up toward the tennis courts. I thought, they were either Highlander Way Middle School students (but tall for middle school) who forgot to get off the bus by their building or they were going to smoke or skip. I had waited until all the buses left, then crossed the service drive and headed towards the courts. I could see two small bits of light inside the wooded area and knew it was a smoke they had decided to sneak in before school. I walked into the little cove of trees and startled the smokers. They hurriedly turned and threw down their cigarettes then back around to face me. I instantly recognized 'Sandy' from her elementary days because I had helped out on the playground at the school she had attended. The young man's face was not familiar to me. I picked up the thrown away cigarettes and asked them to head toward the administrator's office with me following right behind.

No one likes to go through the halls with a security team member following behind them, especially 'Mean Scary Mary.' I sat them down in the office, explained to the administrator what had happened, and left to go back to work.

A few weeks later I was doing bathroom checks when I noticed puffs of smoke coming out of the end stall. I knocked on the stall and told them to open the door. The toilet flushed and three girls emerged from the stall, 'Sandy' and two other females. The third girl coming out looked at me and actually asked me, "What's up?" "Not much, I stated, let's go." As we headed towards the administrators' offices the same girl turned around and asked me why I was taking them down to the office, "We were just talking," she said. I had them sit down, and explained to the administrator what I had found and headed back to work.

Around a week later I noticed a car in the parking lot running during third hour so I went to investigate. I found two students sitting inside – 'Sandy' (Are you kidding me I thought to myself.) and the same young man from the bus incident. I called an administrator who came out to talk to the skippers and investigate the smell coming from the car. When the search was done I headed back to work thinking 'Sandy' was probably going to be in big trouble with her parents. I couldn't ever remember writing a referral on 'Sandy' before, and now three in a matter of weeks.

To my surprise I was called into the office the next day to find out that a complaint had been filed against me. 'Sandy's' mom put in a complaint about me stalking her daughter. "Really? You've got to be kidding me," I replied. When the students were in the smoking pit from the bus, initially I couldn't even tell if they were male or female. The only thing I knew for sure is that one was short and the other was tall. When I walked into the girls' bathroom and caught her smoking I had no idea who was in the stall. The car was being looked at because it was running during the day when everyone should have been in class. Stalking, come on, really? Yes, I know I have written her up three times lately, but maybe mom should have found out what was going on with her daughter. Start with that instead of insinuating that I am the reason her daughter kept getting in trouble. I was really bothered by this one because I knew the parents, and I would think they knew me better than that. Stalking, really?

Chapter Seventeen

A Really Bad Decision

As long as I'm working in any capacity for the school district, I often revert back to my security days. If I see something that strikes me as wrong, I will question it.

I was coming in for afternoon games, and as I was parking in my normal spot, two boys appeared in the lot. It was class time so the students should have been in class plus it was not a student lot. "Hi guys, what are you doing?" I said. "Just showing my buddy my new car," he said, as he walked past me and gave me a 'what's it to you' stare. I responded, "Well, I need to know if you have a pass to be out here during class time?" He replied, "No, we just ran out for a minute. We'll go back in soon." I am thinking, soon, what does that mean? "Second question I have to ask, why are you parking in this lot? What lot is your parking pass for?" I asked. He said, "I just bought my car a few days ago." I am thinking, what is a few? Two days? Three days?

A week? "I haven't had time to get one yet," he said. "I see you haven't had time to get plates yet either," I said. "I am waiting for insurance," he said as he rolled his eyes at me. He was tired and annoyed at my questions. I called security and reported two skippers and a car parked with no plates. The Resource Officer appeared with a security team member, and I proceeded to leave and get ready for my evening event. Apparently, he made a really bad decision to drive his newly purchased car without following a few required steps to put that car legally on the road. Now before he gets insurance and plates he needs to pay for a ticket. Not sure what he regrets more: skipping, parking in the wrong lot, no plates, or rolling his eyes at 'Mean Scary Mary' which caused her to keep questioning him. I think all of the above.

Chapter Eighteen

Mom's Cell

I've met a lot of parents over the years that would say, "Hey keep an eye on my kid. Call me if they do anything stupid." Very few actually gave me their cell phone numbers.

One day I was patrolling the green lot when I noticed four students hustle out the side door by the auditorium and into a truck. I came around the corner, parked, and went to question the students as the came out the aisle of cars. The truck approached and as I put my hand up for them to stop, they swerved around me. The other three boys had ducked down. I saw no faces except for the driver. He was on the opposite side of the vehicle from me, so I didn't get a great view of his face. The license plate was a totally different story.

The truck drove by, and I was getting ready to call the number over the radio, so I didn't forget it. I wouldn't forget this plate because it was a personalized plate. I was almost sure I knew who the driver was after seeing the name on the plate and the glimpse of the student as he avoided me. Realizing who the truck's owner was, I grabbed my phone and called his mom.

I explained to her that 'Steve' left school grounds and he avoided me as I tried to stop him. She informed me that 'Steve' had an appointment that day, but after looking at her watch she said, "Yeah, he's really leaving early." I stated, "He also had three other boys with him." She replied, "He will be right back." Ten minutes later 'Steve' shows back up at school with his friends. Twenty minutes later 'Steve' signed out and left for his appointment.

Chapter Nineteen

The Snow Game

I have had the pleasure of working with good people in the Athletic Department over the years. Because Howell is centrally located in the state, with very nice facilities, we have been asked to host a lot of sporting events. When you put the two together we have hosted a lot of different playoff sports and we do a good job. The most memorable game for me was a state semi-final football game. Not exactly sure who was playing but it really didn't matter, all I can remember was the SNOW.

The prediction was some light snow early with a possibility of heavy snow later in the evening. The game was scheduled for one o'clock, so I wasn't worried. I arrived to help set up and prepared to open the gates. Grounds had been busy clearing the field and stands of the little snow that had accumulated, and it was almost game time. The snow started to come down a little heavier so the Athletic Director at the time, Dan, asked if I could go to the hardware store and get some extra shovels just in case the snow came down a little heavier. My game co-worker and I headed to town and came back with eight shovels. We explained to Dan that we bought every good shovel they had left as the snow started to get heavier.

The teams were ready for the kick-off. We assigned a shovel and a volunteer to every yard line. I took the forty-yard line on the north end of the stadium. The first half wasn't too bad, we could make one walk across and clear most of the snow. Quarters three and four were a different story. I could not make it all the way across the field between plays pushing all that snow. When the teams broke the huddles we would stop and scamper off the field. When the play stopped we would run back onto the field to start where we had left off and try to shovel the rest of the way to the other sideline.

Okay, why wasn't the game stopped I can hear you asking? The winner had to be ready for Ford Field the next weekend and both teams traveled a good distance to get to Howell to play. The snow was also predicted to be heavier the next day so it could have been worse to postpone it.

I felt the final score was pretty low, but the winning team was elated. We were very thankful for the dads' from both teams, and the Howell football coach for manning a shovel so the athletes could get the game completed.

Amanda my daughter, who lives a few hours away, called and asked how my day was going with a chuckle. Jack my grandson was watching TV and saw the highlights from the playoff games and yelled to his mom, "Grandma's on TV shoveling snow at a football game." They backed it up to pause it to take a picture of me and sent it to my phone. So if you think I'm telling a 'big fish story' where a fish grows three to four inches from the actual measurement, the proof is in the picture.

MEAN SCARY MARY | 89

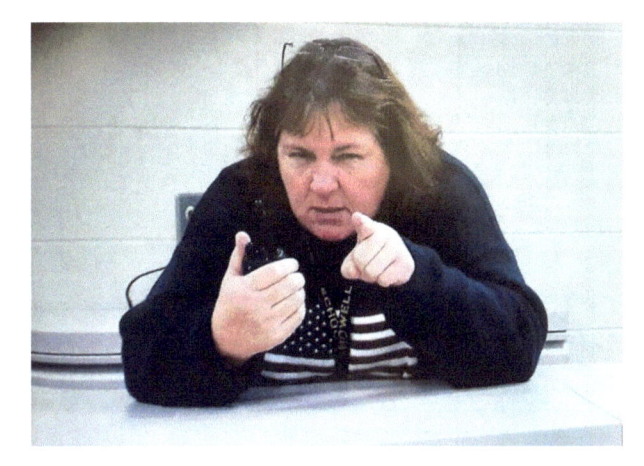

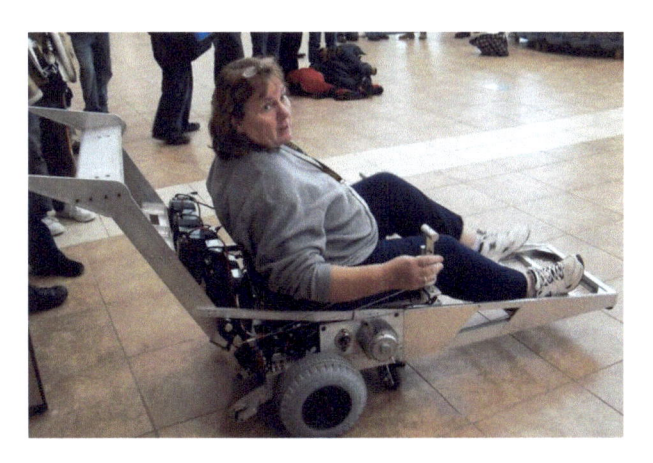

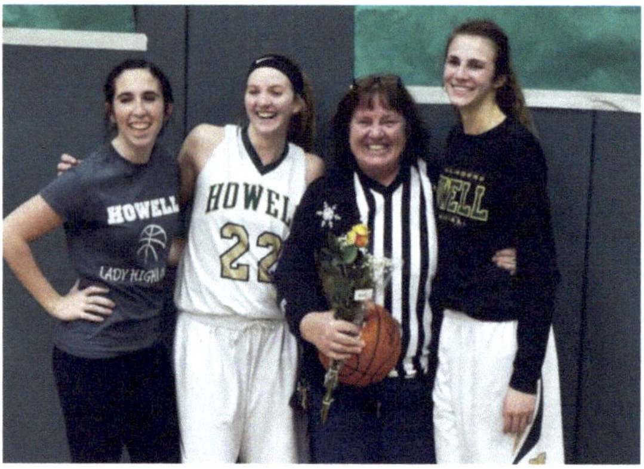
HOWELL
HOWELL
22

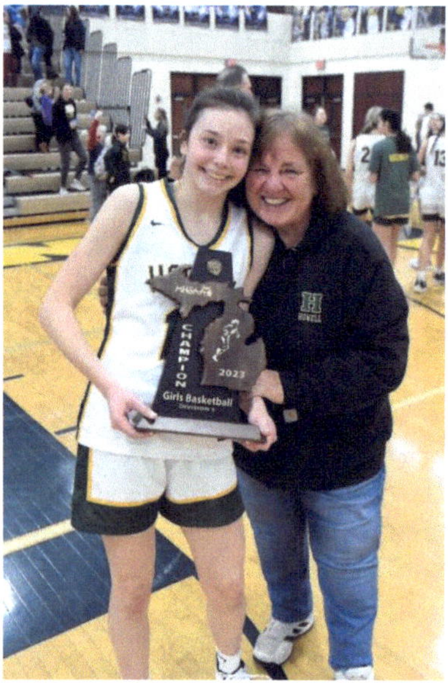
CHAMPION
2023
Girls Basketball

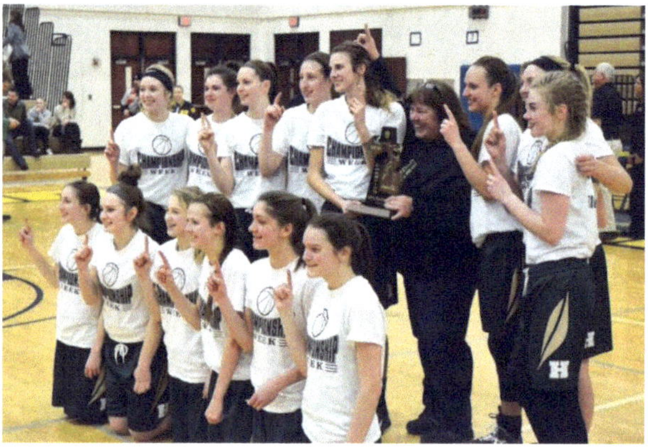

MEAN SCARY MARY | 91

92 | MARY BENEAR

Mary's Work Wisdom and Common Courtesies

Sporting Events, Dance Recitals, Plays, and most Extra Curricular Activities Cost MONEY so Plan Ahead

Remember when going to any of these events you will probably be paying money for them to participate, and for you and family members to attend. Plan for it, and remember to bring some form of payment with you to the event for entrance fees.

If you need to cut back on some things during the year so you can afford to support your child or children and allow them to participate in extra activities that will give them countless memories, I say, "Do it!" I know it can get expensive. To take some of the pressure off, take the time to come up with a savings plan.

They are only young for a few precious years and that time will fly by so plan ahead, and enjoy supporting them in their choice of activities. They are only young for a few precious years and that time will fly by so plan ahead, and enjoy supporting them in their choice of activities.

Chapter Twenty

The Longest Day

Over the years we have had plenty of big athletic events hosted at Howell High. Play-off football games to State Finals in Lacrosse and everything in between. I always try to be available to work the big events; it's the 'all hands on deck' approach.

When I saw wrestling come across my calendar, I wasn't concerned at all. Howell has always had a strong wrestling program with good parent participation. The event was a statewide event (Finals, if I am remembering correctly.) for middle school aged kids and on down to the little wrestlers.

I had arrived early in the morning and things seemed to be running as planned. It was not a Howell Public Schools event, so I did not have to worry about gate money which took a lot of pressure off of me. Wrestling staff and parents were out in full force handling a lot of the behind-the-scenes activities necessary for a smoothly running event. Coach M had decided to cook pancakes in the cafeteria and serve all day breakfast as a fundraiser. He had also brought in a hot dog vendor to help relieve some of the pressure on the concession stand.

A Full House…

They started off with the Parade of Athlete's, and they kept coming and coming. I had never been involved with this group before. I was totally impressed with the participation at this level of competition. You can fit a lot of little wrestlers in a big gym like ours because they take up less room, but where did they all come from? Combining all the parents, little brothers and sisters, proud grandparents, and coaches, made us a full house. Over capacity is bad. I'm unsure about the actual number of people in the gym and cafeteria areas, but would guess we could have been over that day – maybe way over.

I proudly wore my green & gold attire (my family is pretty sure that is all I have in my wardrobe), and my school hang tag identification (ID). I knew my ID would show attendees that they could ask me questions or give me their concerns and I would help them.

Adults Ignore School Policy…

Adults were smoking right outside the doors, so I had stepped outside to remind them that there was no smoking on school grounds. I received the normal response of, "Oh I didn't know that," and the rolling of the eyes like who are YOU trying to enforce the rules. Most people obliged and put their cigarettes out, but some just headed to the parking lots. Still school grounds I bellowed, but my attention had turned to the long line coming out of the cafeteria.

Food…

I walked into the high school and saw the line was for pancakes. Coach M and a wrestler's dad were flipping pancakes as fast as they could. There were four big griddles side by side and they couldn't keep up. I noticed the hot dog vendor was getting a delivery of buns and dogs and his line was also growing long. I decided if I stayed any longer they would want help so I headed back to the gym where I was assigned. When I reached the door 'Matt', a senior wrestler, was carrying three bags of syrup and pancake mix. I held the door for him and we exchanged smiles.

When I walked back into the fieldhouse it happened – the rest of the day was a gigantic blur:

Questions/Requests Never End…

"Ma'am can you help me find a place to change my baby's diaper – I need a table."

"…I need a trainer."

"…Where's the closest ATM?"

"…Where's mat 8, I can't find it."

"…Have you seen a little blond-haired girl with pigtails? I can't find her."

"…When do the finals start?"

"…Do you have any ones, the concession stand is out?"

"…Where's the trainer?"

"…I need a microwave."

"… Where can I buy a souvenir shirt?"

"… Do you have any aspirin?"

"…Who's in charge? I have an issue."

"…Where can I smoke? Where is it not considered school grounds?"

"…Can I borrow some paper and pencils?"

"…Do you have any extra chairs? I can't climb up those bleachers."

"…Can you stop those kids from running in the halls?"

"…I need a trainer."

"…They need change in the cafeteria."

"…Do you have any tape?"

"…Where can I get a salad?"

"…My son lost his cup, where can I get one?"

"…Bathroom has no toilet paper."

"…Do you have any paper towels? I spilled a big drink by the bleachers."

"… If my grandson has lost twice, is he done?"

"…There are kids throwing a football in the hallway."

"…Trash bins are overflowing in the cafeteria. Can you find someone to empty them?"

"…My son Joey lost his match did he come by here crying? Which way did he go?"

"…Where's the trainer?" FOR THE 100th TIME!

"…"

"…"

You can't help everyone and work miracles, but we tried that day to make things run as smoothly as possible with that many people. After a few more impossible to answer questions or demands that couldn't be met, like "…can you find my kid's shoes," I headed back over to the cafeteria and saw a blank look on Coach M's face, like he was beyond whipped. Our eyes met, I pointed at him as I took my ID tag off and said, "I don't think I can ever work this event again." He responded, "Don't worry, we'll probably never host again."

Don't get me wrong, the event was a success. Winners were all smiles, medals were being worn proudly by them and the runners up, and grandparents were walking out with the little ones as they talked a mile a minute smiling ear to ear.

We behind-the-scenes workers were thrilled the day was over without any major problems. Even though Coach M has retired we see each other once in a while. We can both smile and laugh about our longest day ever.

Chapter Twenty-one

The Ticket

    Anyone who really knows me can probably tell you that I have a few favorite things I enjoy doing. Watching any sports (especially my kids and grandkids playing them), playing cards, following the Detroit Tigers baseball team, time with friends, and an occasional trip to the casino. Occasional is all in the eye of the observer.

    It was a mild summer evening as I exited the casino and jumped into my car for the hour ride home. Usually, I would talk to my Aunt Joyce all the way home but leaving at 2:30 in the morning was even a little late, or early depending on perspective, for her. I was enjoying my ride home after a very productive night, again depending on perspective, at the casino by listening to a sports talk radio show talking about my Detroit Tigers. It was a national talk show. They were saying the Tigers needed to trade a few of our key players now to become relevant in a few years. I did not agree with the host and was trying to get them to understand that the trade would be terrible for the Tigers. My voice had elevated in volume, and I was talking a little bit with my hand waving like somehow they could hear me.

As I passed the town of Novi, I noticed a police officer sitting by the exit ramp. There was no one else on the express-way; he's going to have a boring night I thought as I passed him. I took a drink of water and continued to explain to the radio personality that they had no idea what the trade they suggested would do to the Tigers. Wasn't sure how long his light was on when I noticed he was pulling me over, really? I pulled off the highway to the shoulder wondering what I did wrong; the only explanation I came up with is somehow he saw me take a drink. Stay calm I told myself, he probably thinks you have been drinking and I'm sure I looked a little funny if he could see me talking with my hands.

The police officer approached my open window and said, "I need your driver's license and registration, please." "Yes sir, I replied. It's underneath my passenger seat. I need to retrieve my purse." "Okay, he replied, where are you coming from?" "The casino," I answered. I found my wallet and pulled out my driver's license and opened the glove box to find my registration, but I couldn't wait any longer. I turned toward the police officer and said, "Sir, can you tell me what I was doing because this is water, I promise I haven't been drinking."

"You were doing 85 mph," he stated. Wow, didn't expect that! "Sorry, I replied. I didn't even know I was going that fast." The officer answered, "I know because usually when people pass a patrol car speeding, they brake to slow down. You never touched your brakes. By the time I caught up to you, I recorded you at 87." Uh-oh I'm in trouble, no excuses, I was so concentrated on the radio talk show that I never even looked at my speed. There was no traffic to worry about, so I guess I was just flying for me.

I know I have a small lead foot, but I've only received one speeding ticket in recent memories. Thanks Don B. Don didn't issue the ticket, but I was getting lunch for Don when I was pulled over, heavy sigh.

I was handing the officer my driver's license and proof of insurance and he stated, "Do you still live north of Howell?" "Yes," I replied. Strange I was thinking he hadn't even seen my license yet. Maybe he ran my plates as he pulled me over and saw my address, but I know that it does not say my street address is north of Howell on the registration. Now I was a little weirded out as he walked back to his patrol car to run my license and write my ticket, 87 mph Mary, really?

Seemed like I waited forever, but soon he returned to my car window and said "Well 'Mean Mary', you gave me a break my senior year so I'm going to give you a break. Slow down." As a grin filled my face, I asked him his name and what year he had graduated. He replied and I informed him that somehow 'Mean Mary' had turned into 'Scary Mary'. We reminisced about Howell High then I congratulated him on having a good job servicing the community and drove away ticket free.

Chapter Twenty-two

Fights, Fights

Fights, some years we seemed to have multiple confrontations that would lead to slaps, hair pulls, pushes, and flat-out punches being landed. I can also remember some years there would be very few fights, and none of them were considered to be 'big' fights.

Fights happened for many reasons, but none of them were remotely acceptable on school grounds, or anywhere for that matter.

Fight Reasons Don't Fly…

Someone talked about me,
boys,
jealousy,
ex-boyfriend dating someone new,
called me a bitch,
he bumped into me,

said something about my friend,

gave me a dirty look,

have new friends and left me,

took me out during a game in gym class, and again

boys.

Believe me when I say, the security staff have heard it all.

Guy Fights…

They can and usually do happen in an instant. Over the years we have had plenty of them suddenly happen and then abruptly end. Most fights we hear about after the action is over. Then you have to go retrieve the tapes and the participants and take them to the office. Over the radio we hear, "Fight in the Commons," and everyone heads that way. Usually, you can yell at them to stop, and they will comply. Sometimes their pride or egos take over, and they continue to throw punches.

I've stepped into a fight before and was physically shoved by a student. As soon as he realized it was me, he backed off and apologized. I was talked to afterwards about not getting myself involved in fight intervention to quite that level. That's hard for me. The student on the bottom was getting the worst end of the deal.

Some students' emotions were so escalated after a fight that it was hard to calm them down. I would have to professionally hold on to some arms as I escorted them to the office because I couldn't trust them not to use them to return to fighting. They would look at me and say, "Hey, you shouldn't be touching me," funny hearing that coming from someone who just laid a kid out on the ground. After most guy fights you would not hear about it again. Completely a different story with most girl fights.

Girl Fights...

Most of the time you hear about a girl fight for days ahead of the possible altercation. When we hear about a potential fight, we inform the administrators and they call both sides down to try and resolve the situation. Sometimes it works because I really think most girls would prefer not to physically fight. When girl fights do happen, they can be brutal to watch, just not normal. There are so many cameras around the school now that it is easy to find video to watch the fights to get a better understanding of what had transpired. In earlier years, we had to go by what the eyewitnesses said about the fight, and usually there were many different points of view. Before the fight happens most girls assemble a posse of friends to have their back. When we finally arrive at the reason for why the fight even happened, it could take hours of investigation. We are always worried about retaliation so we would have to watch the whole posse for days.

We spent one year at Parker Middle School while they were renovating the high school. Parker was smaller than the Howell High School building, so we had to make adjustments. They created split shifts to accommodate the number of students who attended Howell High. Security hours changed to match the school day hours. I loved it, once a week I could take a day off. Fridays were my choice because there were a lot of sporting events held that day.

Many fights are planned ahead so we usually have to push our way through a crowd of kids. It's surprising how fast a crowd can gather when a fight breaks out. One of the biggest girl fights was at Parker. We knew a particular group of girls were having issues and they had already been talked to in an effort to try to resolve the situation. It finally came to punches and hair pulling on my day off. From what I had heard it was awful. They actually said they decided to ambush the girl that day because 'Mean Scary Mary' wasn't there. I don't know if that was just a story they told or if it was really planned that way. Although I missed that fight, I was at one of the messiest fights over my twenty-year tenure on the security team.

Food Fight...

It was towards the end of the school year; late May, and I had lunch duty on that particular day. I remember what was on the lunch menu – spaghetti, and lots of it. C lunch was usually the busiest of the three lunch periods every day. The lunchroom was rather loud, but that was not unusual. I did notice that the line was extremely long for the main food line. I was sure it was just taking a little longer to dish out spaghetti. A student that usually didn't talk to me much came up and asked me a couple of weird questions. He walked away and it happened, someone yelled, and then all spaghetti hell broke loose. I can honestly say I had never been involved in a food fight before that one, and I sincerely hope I never am again.

Food was flying all over the place. No one must have eaten much of their spaghetti because full plates were being thrown. I was in front of the Kilt Shack, Howell High's spirit wear shop, and called for help over the radio. Over the years I have been told that I come across the radio a little loud or overexcited sometimes, I am sure that day was no exception. I turned around and took a bagel to the side of the head from someone who put some muscle behind it. There were a couple of tables flipped over and on their sides with students hiding behind and underneath them. I found a couple of the ringleaders as did other team members and off to the office we went.

When I went back to the cafeteria, kitchen staff, custodians, and students were cleaning up the mess. I'm sure some of you are laughing about a little food fight, but when it was happening it was awful. Students were getting bombarded with food being whipped at them. To some of the students lining the outer edges of the cafeteria I'm sure it looked like fun. Talk to the kids that were caught in the middle of the chaos and they would tell you they were not laughing. Found out later it was said to be a senior prank.

Every year the administrators tell the seniors – if you do anything that gets you in trouble during the fourth quarter you take the chance of not walking at graduation. I have personally reminded seniors not to do anything stupid and ruin their parents' chance to see them walk across that stage at graduation.

Some of the ringleaders were given the news that they could not participate in graduation. I know some of those seniors made special deals to do community service hours so they could walk. Even after all of the warnings, some students and parents complained that they didn't know that rule.

Chapter Twenty-three

Helping Hands

Most students would help the security staff out if they were asked to help. Over the years incidents have happened and students would help solve some of the mysteries relating to them, especially if it was a serious incident. Cooperation between the students and the security staff is the reason a lot of mystery occurrences have been solved, and mystery students have been identified. Don't get me wrong, some students when asked to help would look at you with that 'yeah right' look. As long as you could keep their name out of it, most kids were very helpful.

Working in the cafeteria one day at lunchtime I noticed a student take something from the lunch cart and walk past the cash register. He noticed I saw him and bolted out the door. We had a few cameras at that time but not many. I headed out the door. He wasn't running down the hall, so I took the stairs and headed up. When I reached the top of the stairs and rounded the corner, he was nowhere in sight. Looking down the hall to the left a student was pointing toward the first classroom door.

    I opened the door to find the teacher writing on the chalkboard looking a little confused about what was happening. He pointed towards the back of his classroom. I approached the back of the room to find a student holding up a newspaper to cover his face. I tapped on the front of the paper; he lowered it, and just stared at me. I pointed to the door. He walked out with me, and never said a word. I would not have found him without the help of the pointing hand.

Chapter Twenty-four

Lawn Jobs

Over the years I have witnessed countless numbers of cars and trucks driving across the lawns and fields at the high school complex. People who don't want to wait in lines to exit or students purposely wanting to see how much damage they can do to the grass while showing off for friends can ruin school grounds. It happens after school hours, so you know they just want to be mischievous. Your character shows up when no one is watching.

During football game nights people will park everywhere. I just have to look the other way sometimes which is hard for me to do. However, parking on the grass is very different than purposely driving across practice fields just to avoid traffic. After one football game I chased (literally) a car across the practice fields getting close enough to get a partial license plate number. With me knowing the color of the car and a partial plate number I started looking every day for that vehicle. When I drove the parking lots, I kept checking every car that matched the color. My husband is an old car buff and can tell you what year and make a car is when it drives by. Other security team members can tell you what kind of car it is from a distance. I can tell you the color! Having had no luck for a week, I believed most people are creatures of habit, so I was hoping to find them after Friday night's game. I was on my gator, sort of hidden, waiting for my 'practice field bandit'. They never showed up that night. Maybe they realized the grounds guys had added rocks to the edge of the fields to deter the drivers from cutting across the fields. 'Mean Scary Mary' doesn't give up easily. It is possible that they had encountered me before, and knew I would be watching after the game. Weeks later I noticed a car parked near the football stadium, same color and a perfect match to my partial license plate number. I asked some of the coaches if they knew who drove that car, a name was given. Fantastic! He was pre-warned that Mary had figured out it was him. I found out there were a lot of chuckles over whether 'Mean Scary Mary' would ever figure it out. It was an adult who was helping out with the football team. He avoided me for days after he knew that 'Mean Scary Mary' had figured out who was driving that car.

The schools' personnel have placed rocks and barriers at strategic places to protect fields and grassy areas. One day after school students had been driving up behind the baseball and softball fields and through the old gravel lot to exit onto the adjacent road to avoid lines. After complaints came to us from the business whose parking lot was used as an exit to Byron Road, we had to start monitoring. When students approached our security team members they were very disgusted that they were asked to turn around to go back to the proper exits. Some days a police officer was writing tickets as the cars came over the dirt and entered the private parking lots. I so wished I could have seen the face of one mom as she yelled at her son, "You said it was okay and that everyone was using this new exit," as she was waiting for her ticket to be written. I won't mention her name because she was well known by the Howell school community. The new exit was soon closed after a few tickets and loads of dirt had been placed at the end of the lot. Message received.

Whether or not it is students, parents, or school employees driving across the grass it can cause damage that isn't always visible. I helped mow lawns at the schools for a short time in the spring of 2022 for the grounds department at the high school. I instantly realized the ruts left by the tires are hard to see but you felt them immediately. So please remember that someone has to fix the ruts your car creates, or someone's back suffers when they mow over them.

Chapter Twenty-five

Mailboxes

If I knew then what I know now, before I started my security job, I would have purchased stock in mailboxes. Over my years of enforcing rules at the high school we have lost approximately 17 mailboxes.

They have been smashed, shot, stolen, and one was even blown up. "Really?" some would say. My husband would ask, "Who did you bust lately," whenever he had to replace a mailbox. One mailbox was a random act because three other neighbors lost their mailboxes on the same night. We assumed one was taken out by a drunk driver because he left some of his truck mirror and headlight by our smashed mailbox. One was over a family dispute because I found out later that the young man bragged about shooting our mailbox. The student that told me about it didn't want to get involved because he couldn't trust the kid not to retaliate against him.

The rest of the havoc wreaked on our mailboxes had no explanation. My neighbors couldn't understand how our mailbox was the only one in the neighborhood to be smashed or just gone. My husband found certain, less upsetting, ways to tell me if the mailbox disappeared overnight. Usually it was, "If you're going anywhere after work pick up another mailbox," said with a grin. Sometimes Jeff would be able to straighten them out so that they were still usable, not great looking but it would open and close. My regular mail-carrier actually felt bad for me and delivered the mail up to the house a few times.

The worst was when my son-in-law made me a mailbox that would swivel when someone hit it hard with a bat. After two attempts to ruin the box, they just came back and stole the whole mailbox.

One time our mailbox was actually blown-up. Not many people would believe that story except the kids ended up blowing a hole in the floorboard of their truck. They needed medical attention and admitted to blowing up my mailbox along with some others on an adjoining road.

Hopefully now that I'm retired from security (only subbing once in a while) they will leave our brand-new shiny mailbox alone.

PLEASE!

Chapter Twenty-six

Loud Voice

Over the years, I have never been accused of having a quiet meek voice. It makes for a very good *bingo* caller or for getting everyone's attention at a family gathering.

I was a little league coach for a few years, and it really helped in getting the attention of twelve or thirteen little five- to eight-year-olds. One year after my team's first practice, I had a grandmother remove her grandson off my team because of my loud voice. Apparently, I was loud like the youngster's mother with whom they were having difficulties. I had always thought that it was because I was a woman coach, and she was not having her grandson on the only woman-coached team. My team had a pretty good year, so I was invited to be an All-Star coach. It was tryout day, and the grandmother and her grandson showed up for the tryouts. She motioned me over, and asked if we could talk. She was hoping that I wouldn't hold it against her little one because she had pulled him off my team. "Absolutely not," I responded, but I told her that I still had a loud voice. He made the team.

In my years of working security my loud voice has come in handy. When I was in a hallway and there were some kids horse-playing at the other end of the hall I would yell and get their attention. I did have one administrator suggest I should lower my voice when I was dealing with students. Such as it is, this is my normal voice.

Through the years some students thought I was yelling at them and would complain. I usually responded with letting them hear my elevated voice, "THIS IS ME YELLING!" So, when students tell me they didn't hear me, I call it selective hearing.

Usually, kids had fair warning of where 'Mean Scary Mary' was, because they could hear the clatter of my keys or my loud voice. I eventually learned that the element of surprise was important, so I learned how to be quieter. Over the years, the surprised looks on students' faces when I would just appear out of nowhere were priceless.

Chapter Twenty-seven

The Scream

Throughout my stories I have mentioned my loud voice plenty of times. I have even written a chapter about it. 😊 At one point, an administrator suggested that maybe I could bring down the volume when I speak, really? That would be like asking a soft voiced person to speak louder all the time, it is not natural. I was given this voice and I am not going to try to change it now. Most people have a distinguished laugh that is uniquely theirs. They would have to consciously change their laugh, like an actor, where is the spontaneity in trying to do that? Your voice and laugh make you who you are; there is no point in trying to change them.

Over the years my loud voice has come in handy. When I had called *bingo* in a hall before, I received positive feedback from those in attendance. I have attended gatherings where there is no microphone available and have been asked to get everyone's attention

– no problem. I have hardly ever been asked to speak up because someone cannot hear me. Each one of us has many characteristics that make us who we are; one of mine is my loud voice.

'The SCREAM' has been used over the years on special occasions. After a big win, the players and coaches would be going over the game in the locker room. When they first enter you usually hear loud celebrating and then it gets really quiet. That is when the coach is usually telling the team how proud he or she is of their strong effort and their resilience. Especially if they fought from behind in a big rival game, he or she tells them that this is what all their hard work accomplished.

I wait until that quiet time and then I run in and let it rip. I SCREAM! I explain how proud I am of the team and that it was awesome to watch them fight as I go around and high-five everyone. Then I leave as quickly as I came in. On a rare occasion, I have even let 'the SCREAM' out in an away locker room which is really special.

I have never asked permission from the coaches, so it is also a surprise to them. I have been told by a coach that the first time he heard 'the SCREAM' he almost had a heart-attack. Now he keeps an eye on the door during his post-game talks, especially after a big game. I've even unloaded 'the SCREAM' in the men's locker room. I'll check with an assistant coach to make sure everything is clear before I surprise the team. The coaches never seem to mind me interrupting their speech to let out 'the SCREAM!'

If they do mind, I have never been told to quit. 'The SCREAM' has always been reserved for Varsity Teams until recently.

At the end of the 2022 basketball season, the boy's Junior Varsity (JV) team was hosting Okemos. I was sitting at the head table and didn't have many interruptions, so I really enjoyed watching a total team effort for a come from behind win. We were down around 18 points or so, and they just kept working hard. I was impressed with this young team's composure during their hard-fought comeback. Honestly, I can't tell you who scored the winning basket but it doesn't matter, it was a true team win.

I decided to make my first ever JV Boys SCREAM visit. I had received a thumbs up from an assistant coach so I went in, gave 'the SCREAM' and high-fives all around, then left. Later that same month the freshman boys' team came from behind for a great win over a quality team. Why not 'the SCREAM' I thought. When I entered the locker room and let out 'the SCREAM' at first the guys seemed confused. I finally explained to them how impressed I was with them never giving up and how hard they fought to get that win. That's why you never give up, yells came, high-fives all around and then I left.

The JV girls' team had an awesome come from behind win in January of 2023. We were hosting Brighton when the girls found themselves behind by double digits and the Brighton crowd was unusually loud. They kept clawing their way back into the game and pulled out a quality win. I was headed to the locker room when I passed the coaches already leaving but the girls had a great reaction to 'the SCREAM'. It always makes it special when they beat a rival. I just hoped the Varsity boys' team had heard 'the SCREAM' in Brighton when I announced to the Howell crowd that they had had an over-time win beating the Bulldogs to end the Brighton winning streak.

Not sure how many years I have left in the Howell Athletic Department, so I hope I get a few more chances to let out 'the SCREAM!'

Chapter Twenty-eight

Apology Hug

Three students came in from the front parking lot and I greeted them at the front door. "Hey guys where are you coming from?" I asked. As I mentioned before, when you have a group of students, one student does all the talking so the story doesn't change. 'Jimmy' did all the talking with this group. "We were at the Freshman Campus and Mr. S kept us after so we're running late." I let them go after taking all of their names, that story is easy to check out. First of all, they shouldn't have been driving to the Freshman Campus and secondly, 'Jimmy' could hardly keep eye contact with me. I called the Freshman Campus to leave a message for Mr. S and quickly found out that he was sick and didn't come to work that day.

I called 'Jimmy' down later and explained to him that he needed to have a better excuse or at least use a teacher's name that was actually at work. "Sorry," he said, can I give you an apology hug for lying to you?" That's different I thought. "Sure," I said. After a quick hug he grins and says, "Well technically you didn't catch us." "Well, I said, you can consider this referral a technicality because you did get caught!"

Chapter Twenty-nine

No Handshake

  Parents of 'Olivia' thought my security partner and I were picking on their daughter. Within a seven-week period, we either took her to the office or wrote referral after referral. We were always catching her and 'John,' her boyfriend, skipping or being in an unauthorized area. We would commonly find them in parking lots, the fieldhouse, and back halls as we made our rounds.

  My security partner and I were informed by an assistant principal that we had been asked to come to their office after lunch for a meeting with 'Olivia's' parents. We knew that it would probably be uncomfortable for everyone included, but we had nothing to hide. We had never written her up for being in class.

  'Dennis' and I walked into the office, and I extended my hand to introduce myself. 'Olivia's' dad refused to acknowledge my attempt to greet him, turned his back on us, and sat down. Dennis said, "Let's go Mary; we are not going to have a conversation with someone who has no common courtesy. Maybe he should talk to his daughter about being out of class all the time." We walked out and never heard another word about it.

Chapter Thirty

Small World

It's surprising how many places you can go and run into someone you know; local grocery stores, restaurants, gyms, and gas stations don't count, you almost expect to see someone you know locally.

What are the Odds…

I was in Las Vegas in March one year walking through a casino down a row of slot machines and I thought I heard a familiar voice. I turned around and there was a Kensington Valley Conference (KVC) head basketball coach. He was enjoying time with some family members as I tapped him on the shoulder. We ended up meeting up later for some beverages, and enjoyed some good conversation off the gym floor.

Beating the Odds…

My group of four people were headed out of Metro Airport for a trip to Las Vegas for a long weekend when a Howell High teacher/coach walked by our table. We exchanged pleasantries and hugs and found out he was headed to California to meet his brother. He was landing in Las Vegas and renting a car for the final stage of his trip, and offered to give us a ride to the hotel. He would land approximately twenty minutes before us and would go grab his car and come back to retrieve us. We accepted the awesome gesture since that meant no taxi or bus waiting. When 'Matt' returned to gather us up for our hotel ride, he was in an awesome red convertible. My friend and I had packed pretty lightly, but my daughter and her buddy had a little more luggage. We were quite the sight driving down the strip with five adults and countless bags shoved everywhere, music full blast, and all of us singing at the top of our lungs. 'Matt' gave us the best carpool ride ever.

Chance…

Walking down a path by a river walk in Florida I was telling a story to my sister-in-law. Two bikes rode by and almost immediately stopped. "Mary Benear is that you? 'Ruth' asked. We rode by, and 'Tom' said, I think I just heard Mary Benear." They were camping just down the waterway from where we were staying with Jeff's family. 'Tom' worked at Howell High. It is a small world.

Second Chance…

One of the most unexpected chance encounters I have had was in Myrtle Beach, South Carolina. My daughter invited grandma to go stay with her and the grandkids at a condo for a week. Her husband was called out of town for work, and she was expecting her third child so an extra pair of hands would come in handy. One of the excursions she planned was a visit to a Mermaid/Pirate show. There were two shows per night, and we had tickets to the early show. After a great show and meal, both sides of the theater were rushed out through a double door exit. As around 400 of us (spectators) were going through the exit corridor I heard "Well hello Mrs. Benear." I turned around to see a Howell graduate with his wife and two little ones in tow. He introduced me to his family as one of his favorite security guards and he said he couldn't wait for me to have his little boy at the high school. I shook hands and burst his bubble as I told him I had just retired. I told his little one to play sports and I would see him in the gym. We stepped out into the fresh air, visited for a couple of minutes and then said our goodbyes.

It is definitely a small world.

Chapter Thirty-one

Nieces, Nephews, My Kids

Over my years of security at Howell High, I have had several family members attend the high school. I've always let them make the decision of whether they wanted their friends to know that they were related to 'Mean Scary Mary.' Obviously, my daughters and son had no choice because of their last name. It was hard for them to deny that I am related and their mother. Benear is not a very common name.

Some family members kept their distance, and would just nod and smile when they walked by me in the halls. Others would have no problem making it known that Aunt Mary and 'Mean Scary Mary' are the same Mary. Dana who is my niece would yell down the hall, "Hi Aunt Mary." She would always bring a smile to my face. First because she always seemed so comfortable being herself, she didn't seem to care what other people thought. Students can miss out on having a good high school experience because they are always worrying about what other people might think of them. Second because Dana had inherited some of my <u>LOUD</u> voice.

    My nephew Andrew was having a birthday party his freshman year. Family was invited for the afternoon for cake and his buddies were coming over later for game night. I had plans earlier in the day so my husband and I stopped by on our way home to wish Andrew a happy birthday. We entered the house and found about ten freshmen sitting around the table enjoying pizza with several different conversations going on. When I entered the dining area the chatter level came way down and I heard "What's 'Mean Scary Mary' doing here? Why would she be at your birthday party Andrew?" "She's my Aunt Mary," Andrew stated. You could see the disbelief in some of their faces. PRICELESS!

    At work I was watching students from the top of the main stairs during passing time and noticed a male student showing a lot of friends a card or something. He received some high-fives. I stepped a little closer to note that it was a driver's license being held by my nephew. He turned around, proceeded to come up the main stairs, and noticed me standing there. I just stuck my hand out. He looked at me then finally placed the fake ID in my hand. That led to other fake IDs being confiscated after we saw on camera who was distributing them to other students.

    My youngest daughter said that she never minded me working there when she was a senior. It would come in handy when she needed to leave to grab something she forgot at home. I would just walk to the office and sign her out. Her senior year I have some of the best senior exit pictures because I was working there and had great opportunities to capture the moments. She was written-up (a referral) only once in her high school career and I was called to ID her. She and three friends decided to leave campus for lunch and pick-up something for a project. Someone on the security staff saw them going into the parking lot and came across the radio asking for my help to ID them. I replied, "Yes, I can – Benear, BLANK, and BLANK." They spoke back over the radio asking if I could spell the names for them. "B-E-N-E-A-R," I replied. Later, with a smirk on their faces they asked me what I wanted to do with the lunch-skippers. "It's your referral, write it," I stated. She can handle it when the administrator calls her down.

My oldest daughter graduated before I started on the security team so she only had to deal with me through her athletics. I started in the Athletic Department during her freshman year so she was used to me being around after school hours. My three kids always played two to three sports a year so working with the Athletic Department was great. I was fortunate to never have to hear the scores of their games after they happened because I was always near or in the stands as they happened. They all seemed to enjoy having mom always being at their sporting events.

But when it came to my security job, my son hated it. He was always being told by different people about his mom busting them (like he could do anything about it). He could have cared less about me doing my job, but the students always pointing it out to him became very annoying. One day I had asked him about the grief he took because I was working at the high school. He stated he took some, but he could handle it. I told him that when they complained about me just say, "Hey at least you don't have to live with her." He's always been a strong kid and he can handle anything thrown at him, he just shouldn't have had to because of me.

My niece Rachel told me she would hear stories at the middle school she attended about 'Mean Scary Mary'. Some friends she would tell, "She's my Aunt, you know." Other times she would just laugh. Overall, I think most of them handled being related to 'Mean Scary Mary' pretty well even when it was incognito.

Chapter Thirty-two

Aunt Mary

By: Rachel Salmon

Many of you may not know this but 'Mean Scary Mary' is my aunt. She is my mom's sister, and has always been a huge person in my life. When we all get together, she is the one who is always down to play cards, always willing to tell you stories, and she always makes sure that you've had a sweet treat to eat and plenty to drink.

Growing up in the Howell school district, I knew that my Aunt Mary worked at the high school but wasn't quite sure what her job title was or what she did. I knew that she worked a lot with the Athletic Department and put in her time at the school during the day but that was about it. During middle school people were starting to spread rumors about this mean and scary security guard named Mary. I knew that they were talking about my aunt but couldn't see my funny and witty aunt being that mean or scary. When the rumors got to me I would kind of laugh them off because being Mary's niece I could never see her breaking a kid's arm or chasing after kids or any of the other crazy stories they were telling me. I knew the fun-loving side of her, not the crazy story side that they were describing about her.

  I was always a big rule follower during my school days, and in high school I only ever missed one day of school (it was Senior Skip Day, so of course I wasn't going to be there). I was never in trouble; I did great in school (except Physics, but who needs that?), and was kind of quiet. I was on the high school golf team (Varsity for 3 years) and I was in choir for two years in high school.

  Fast forward, to the end of my senior year of high school. Somehow I had forgotten that on that particular day I had to have all of my textbooks turned in so that I could graduate. I knew that my mom was at work in Southfield and wasn't sure what my dad was doing on the farm, but knew he wouldn't be thrilled if I called him to ask him to bring me the one textbook that I had left at home. Third hour came around and I realized that we had a substitute, and we were just watching a movie for the day. It was Advanced Placement (AP) biology and we had already taken our AP exams. I thought that was my chance to run home, grab the book, and get back without ever having to sign out or call my parents. Granted I live a couple of miles north of the school, but I didn't think it would be that big of a deal. I knew right where the textbook was in my room on the floor.

  The biggest issue that I thought I would have would be sneaking out past my Aunt Mary, driving past her house (on the off chance she might already be home), and then getting back into the school without Aunt Mary getting a glimpse of me. At the time I was driving my family's big old custom 2002 Blue Chevy Astro Van. It was very recognizable and had been in my family for a lot of years. Aunt Mary definitely knew the car and that I was the one driving it because my siblings were all younger than me.

I told a friend of mine in the class what I was doing. I went up to the substitute, and told her that I was not feeling well and needed to go to the bathroom. She allowed me to go, and since I had my keys and ID with me already, I left my backpack and walked out to my car. I was able to sneak out of the school without detection from Aunt Mary. I thought that the hardest part was over. I hoped that if I got caught on my way back into school that I could reason with my Aunt and she would let it go. After all I was a senior, and only had a few days left in school.

I was able to get out of the parking lot and onto M-59 without being detected. I drove straight home, went right upstairs, grabbed my book, and was back in the car in less than 2 minutes. I thought I was doing great!

I was waiting at the stop sign at the end of my road to make a right turn, when a semi came up to the intersection and turned on their turn signal to turn down our road. I will never forget my dad's face as he turned onto our road and realized that I was the one at the stop sign when I was supposed to be in school. Thankfully, I was able to return to school, sneak back in without getting detected by Aunt Mary, and get back into class.

The substitute did ask where I had been because I had been gone for 20 minutes. I told her that my stomach wasn't feeling well, and that I was in the bathroom. She said that she had checked the bathroom, but didn't see me in there. I said that I was in a bathroom further away because the one that was right next to the classroom always stank. Thankfully, she didn't ask me any more questions and allowed me to go to my seat.

I promise that I would never have done this again because the anxiety of possibly getting caught by that 'Mean Scary Mary' security guard was not worth it. Just because she is my funny Aunt, that doesn't mean that she wouldn't have written me up and told my parents about what I had done.

Obviously, my parents did find out what I was doing because that night at supper my dad mentioned seeing me turning at the corner when I was supposed to be in school. They didn't seem to mind too much because I had not gotten into any trouble, and I was trying to do the right thing and return my textbook.

Chapter Thirty-three

Restaurants

I've always enjoyed spending my money at local 'Mom & Pop' restaurants. It brings a smile to my soul when they greet you by name and take the time to welcome you in.

One afternoon as two other school employees and I were eating lunch at one of my favorite local restaurants, sitting at the outside tables were ten of our student athletes. After some discussion the three of us decided to pick up their bill. We informed the waitress of our intentions finished our meals, paid the bills, and greeted the athletes as we left the restaurant. We noticed they were collecting money as we walked by, and it brought a smile to our faces that they would soon find out some strangers had picked up their bills.

The next day at school a few of the students asked if we picked up their lunches. I just smiled and went about my business never admitting it was us. On my next trip to that restaurant, we found out that not only had those athletes cleaned up all their tables and carried all their dishes inside, but we also learned that the money that they had collected to pay their bill they left with the waitress as a tip. The waitress was overwhelmed; she has a son with special needs and was really struggling at the time. Talk about paying it forward.

My husband has a different reaction when he hears them greet me. When he hears "'Mean Scary Mary' is here," he's ready to hit the door. I would tell him, "We're okay they're good kids." Most kids are good, but sometimes they just do something dumb.

I've only walked out of a restaurant once in my twenty years that I've been involved in security. I was with a friend, and I was greeted as I entered to be seated, "Hi 'Scary Mary.'" No big deal, I've heard that name thousands of times before, but after the waitress took our drinks order a familiar face peeked through the kitchen window with a big smirk on his face. I had busted him a few months earlier which ended up in a suspension. He was really upset with me, and I figured the smirk was enough. I paid for our drinks and we exited.

Chapter Thirty-four

Rumors – Rumors – Rumors

Most rumors start off being a little bit accurate until they go through the *'Telephone Game'*. There might be some truth to an event that starts a rumor, but by the time the story travels through a lot of students, the story/rumor ends up not being completely accurate. Some rumors are just started because someone's mad or jealous. Either way the rumors can take on a life of their own.

While I was working at the high school I didn't realize there were so many rumors about me and over the years how much the rumors grew. I'm sure I have never heard all of them, probably glad I haven't, but a few have put a smile on my face.

Community Service…

Some student thought I was an ex-police officer, and I stole drugs and drug money from a bust. At my sentencing the

Judge gave me a stern lecture and community service. I tried to explain I actually get paid to work here and they wouldn't put a criminal in a school system. I'm sure after six years my probation would be over by now. They still didn't believe me so I finally gave up trying to explain myself.

Wow She's Strong…

That came to be because I did a video for 'Matt' his senior year. 'Matt' had me answer pre-determined questions that made me look very strong. After answering all of his questions, 'Matt' edited it into a short video. I don't remember what the title was but some of the questions were…

> …How does it feel to be the strongest women in the world?
> …Who's your hero?
> …Have you ever killed anyone?
> …Would you arm wrestle me?

I had agreed to arm wrestle 'Matt' so we stood over a trash can outside the Media Center. The camera man said 'go' and it was on. It seemed like it took a long time but I prevailed – winner, winner chicken dinner. During the interview I was asked to be real serious but inside it was hard to control my laughter. Then I realized he probably let me win for the sake of the video. Oh well it was fun, and 'Matt' thought it went well.

The video came out and I thought 'Matt' did a great job of putting it together to make me look tough. I walked into the lunch room after the video was shown and students kept asking me to arm wrestle. I kept explaining not today and they kept asking. Finally I gave up and agreed to arm wrestle 'Mike' because he kept asking. Quite a few students gathered around, and I stated, "Win or lose this will be my last match (only my second ever)." 'Mike' sat down at the lunch table as his friends moved to give me space on the other side of the table. It was ON! I was holding my own with 'Mike's' friends hooting and hollering in the background 'Mike' smiled then it was over – winner, winner chicken dinner. I think he was distracted long enough to give me a chance and I took it. Never arm wrestled again.

Fast Fast Fast...

Wow she's faster than she looks. Every time I heard this rumor it would put a smile on my face. Over the years I had figured out patterns students would use to leave campus or sneak back in. I would guess a lot where they were going and cut them off by choosing a short-cut. I really don't see any other reason for 'fast' being associated with 'Mean Scary Mary.'

Broken Arm…

Not sure where or when this rumor started but supposedly I talked to a student, and it was said that during our discussion I broke his arm. I did not break his arm.

Chapter Thirty-five

The Black Bag

One cool fall morning I was driving through the senior lot when I noticed two girls outside a car where one of the girls was throwing up. I parked, got out of my car, and when I approached the ladies there was a very distinct smell in the air. "Ladies, what's up?" I asked. 'Sue' stated, "'Jamie' didn't feel good so we thought we would come out and get some fresh air before first hour started." We were already in third hour so this could be a big problem I thought to myself. "Okay, let's get her inside and warmed up," I replied because I could see 'Jamie' physically shaking. I escorted them to the front office conference room where I left the girls and told them I would be back with some water.

I informed an administrator about what I had witnessed and returned to the conference room carrying waters escorted by the administrator. The minute we opened the door the administrator could tell my suspicions were right. He talked to the ladies and informed them that he would be searching their belongings to make sure they didn't have anything they shouldn't have on school property. He searched their backpacks which were clean and then he turned his attention to a box purse which he found to be locked. 'Sue' indicated it was hers, but she had lost the key. I interrupted her and reminded her that she had put it down her blouse on our walk in. The administrator left the room so the key could be retrieved and the search continued. The purse contained a bag of marijuana so the next step was to make sure the car was clean. The administrator asked 'Sue' to escort us to the car as 'Jamie' was still not looking well. We were informed that the car didn't belong to either girl.

When we received the owner's name I was sent to retrieve her and her keys. I arrived and 'Ann' was taking a test so after a 10 minute wait I escorted her and the car keys to the front parking lot. When it was explained to her that we had found the girls using her car this morning she became instantly angry! "Before school started they asked me if they could have a smoke in my car because it was cold outside. I was being nice and now I'm getting in trouble. Are you kidding me?" 'Ann' asked.

After some explanation from the administrator she unlocked her car and I immediately realized why she was so mad. The stuff we found added up quickly, two packs of cigarettes, a grinder, smoking pipes, and then 'Ann' said, "Okay, I'll give it to you." She opened the glove box and removed a fake top and reached in, removing a bag of marijuana. Wow, I never would have found that I was thinking to myself, when the administrator told 'Ann' to open the trunk. She protested and stated, "I already gave you the bag. Can we just go inside?" The administrator explained that we would be searching the trunk.

'Ann' opened the trunk and the search continued with the discovery of seven bottles of booze, three were half empty and four of them had been purchased for Saturday night's party she informed us. During the time the administrator was pulling out the bottles of booze, I opened a black gym bag and immediately found myself zipping it back up. The administrator asked me what was in the bag, and I informed him that we needed a female administrator. His response was, "Give me the bag." I was given a stern look but held my ground as we loaded everything up and headed inside. When we arrived at the female administrator's office she asked me what was going on. I explained the events of the morning to her, escorted 'Ann' in, and then gave her the bag. I pulled all the contents of the car out of the bag and proceeded to lay them out on her desk as she asked 'Ann,' "Who do you want me to call?" "Mom," she stated. I was asked to sit with 'Ann' while we waited for her mom. We sat in absolute silence.

Ten minutes later, the administrator returned escorting 'Ann's' mom into her office. I felt bad for her mom as she stared with a blank look on her face at everything on the desk: cigarettes, grinder, pipes, marijuana, booze, and then was handed the black bag. Mom, after looking inside the gym bag, decided she needed her husband. She called her husband who was at work and convinced him she needed him to come to the high school. Twenty minutes later dad showed up, and I was excused to leave. A month later I was walking the halls when I walked past 'Ann' and she gave me a slight smile. I asked her how she was doing and she stated things were slowly getting better. She graduated on time with her class and I was truly happy for her. What was in the bag could really have messed things up for her, but usually one mistake in your young life you can overcome. It's how you react to the situation and if you learn from it that can help shape your future. If she hadn't given in to peer pressure that morning and given her friends permission to use her car she might never have been caught. Maybe in the long run it was a good thing we confiscated the bag and everything else in that car on that day, she was definitely going down a bad path.

The bag had some R rated materials and objects inside!

Chapter Thirty-six

'Mean Scary Mary' Facts

For twenty years, there have been 'Mean Scary Mary' rumors swirling around. I hope this chapter will put some of them to rest. Here I give you a few facts that I will verify:

> ...I was honored to be the Grand Marshall at two different Homecoming Parades. One actually happened, the second one was rained out, but it was still awesome to be asked.

> ... During a hockey game I had to restrain a student against the glass who was throwing punches. He calmed down when he noticed it was ME.

> ...My hair was cut off at school during a pep assembly for Ribbon Warriors for Cancer. I didn't have the courage to let them shave it all off, but I went really short.

...I was fortunate to be able to pitch in a Slow-Pitch National Championship in Arizona before I became 'Mean Scary Mary'.

...I have been in a lot of videos over the years for student projects or applications for Senior Survivor. If you have ever seen these videos you know I can definitely make fun of myself.

...One year students from Howell who were attending Michigan State had created a top ten list. You know you're from Howell, Michigan if...

#3. You were ever chased by 'Mean Scary Mary'

#8. You know Mary Benear

...At a playoff hockey game I was sent to supervise our student section and I had to step in between two grown men. Two adults started arguing about something down the row from where I was sitting and it became pretty heated. I decided to walk down there since one of the men was a Howell parent. I actually had to extend my arms and placed my hands on both men's chests. The Howell dad said, "I'm fine Mary." The other guy gave me a dirty look but turned around and left the section.

MEAN SCARY MARY | 153

...One of the longest winning streaks that I have ever heard mentioned...one of the best Livingston County, if not the best, middle school basketball teams was the St. Joseph Crusaders coached by Coach M. In 1994 they did not have enough seventh and eighth graders so his oldest son along with a couple other sixth graders joined the varsity team and the winning started. The team went 43-0 in 1994-95-96. Then his second son joined my son Chris on the varsity team and they went 29-1 in 1997 & 1998. Seventy-two to one speaks for itself.

...I have had to physically restrain a couple of students during my twenty years of being 'Mean Scary Mary'. I was told by one young lady who tried to push through me to exit a space that her lawyer would be contacting me soon. He must have lost my number.

...We were informed one day that the high school and fieldhouse were being evacuated. The voice on the loudspeaker was announcing to everyone that they needed to evacuate the building immediately. School was let out early at 2:00pm and everyone was in the process of leaving when the athletic secretary and I started clearing the fieldhouse. She was informing a student that he needed to leave the fieldhouse when he replied, "Who says I have to leave?" I would have yelled at him if I had told him to leave and he responded like that, but she calmly responded that we were told the power company had called. Before she could get another word out of her mouth, he yelled, "Then it's a gas leak." As he threw his hands up in the air, she replied, "Thanks, 'Captain Obvious.'" We both looked at each other, and I could not quit laughing. It was a priceless response to a smart aleck student, forever to be known as 'Captain Obvious' to the two of us.

...As I was eating at Mark's Coney Island one day I ran into a former female student who I hadn't seen in years. She informed me that she had moved back to Howell a while ago, gotten married, and had two little ones along with a bonus child that kept her busy. We were talking and for some reason getting older came up in our conversation. I told her you just have to welcome getting older with a good mindset. You have to remember the older you get the less you worry or care what other people think of you and some of the silly things you do. You can just be yourself all the time and never worry about being fake to impress anyone. "Mrs. Benear," she said, "you never really cared what people thought of you, you were always just yourself."

She was absolutely right. I never thought I should have to change myself to please other people or that I should have to pretend to be something I wasn't. You get what you get with me, and I totally understand that not everyone is going to like me. Just be yourself and it will be okay. My dad always told me you need to be able to smile at the person you see when you look in the mirror.

Chapter Thirty-seven

Never Off Duty

For some reason I never feel off duty whenever I'm around the school grounds. Between working on the security staff and for the Athletic Department, I seemed to spend a lot of time around and on the school complex.

I could be leaving for lunch when I'm working for the Athletic Department, and I would see students walking off campus. I would pull up to them and ask them where they were going. I would turn them around and then call the security staff and let them know the students were heading back. My lunch partners would smile and put up with me most of the time. Once in a while they would say, "Mary you're at lunch, or you are not security today Mary." I could not pass the skating park during a school day if there were people using it. I would roll down my window and inform them that the skate park is closed till 2:30 pm when school is in session. Some kids were hard of hearing, or their selective hearing would kick in, so I would have to get out of my car and explain to them that during school hours the skate park is closed. Other times I would have to remind them that there is no smoking on school grounds.

I'm constantly directing kids after school to the skate park away from unauthorized areas for skateboarding. I let kids know there is no throwing of balls in the fieldhouse hallways, that they need to take it outside. I can hardly go to a parking lot anywhere without noticing people that have to use extra spots for their cars. Your car is no more important to you than our cars are to us. Leave us a spot! I used to carry the orange stickers with me that we place on cars to let the owner know that they are parking illegally in our lots. (Wrong lot, wrong spot, using too many spaces, etc.) But after being tempted so many times to put a sticker on a car in a private lot I decided to quit carrying them. I have left a note as a friendly reminder that they are no more important than the rest of us!

Even in restaurants during the day, students will avoid eye contact with me because they don't want me to notice them. I have told some groups "Don't worry, I'm off duty." I hope that when I completely retire, I will be able to shut off that part of my brain.

It's not only on our school grounds. I was at the Friday night football game watching Howell's student section when I noticed something. The students at the top of the bleachers were all turned around watching something. I exited the bleachers and went around to the back side of the bleachers. I watched as three of our students were climbing over a pretty high fence to get into the game free. I explained to them that it would have been easier walking through the visitor's gate. I escorted them to the gate and watched them pay with a fifty. Really!

Mary's Work Wisdom and Common Courtesies

Bring Back Homecoming Floats

Students use to take pride in coming up with an idea for a float, then watching it come to life! It would be great if teachers and parents volunteered to help supervise students and local businesses donated supplies so the Howell High School student body can start building floats for Homecoming again.

Chapter Thirty-eight

Senior Pranks

Over the years seniors have been warned not to do anything stupid or bad especially during the fourth quarter. If they are caught during that time period making a big mistake, by doing something dumb, it could possibly stop them from walking with their graduation class. A variety of acts from fighting, excessive skipping, drugs, drinking, or participating in a senior prank can be the reason they're denied senior activities.

Most senior pranks are innocent and are done just for fun but others have gone overboard and caused damage to property or individuals. Senior pranks usually happen within the last week of the seniors attending high school classes. The security staff starts watching a little more intently toward that last couple of weeks that senior attendance is required. Over my twenty year tenure as 'Mean Scary Mary' I had witnessed senior pranks that would be described as mild to pranks that caused a lot of discomfort at the time. The students thought the element of surprise made for some of the best senior pranks.

Deer Scent Urine: What a terrible smell. It started in the back hallways and quickly spread through the entire building. It was so strong in some hallways it brought tears to students eyes. It started off as a slightly sweet odor but smells like ammonia within minutes.

Toilet Paper: Everywhere. Pretty harmless, but made for a messy clean up especially after a small rainstorm. Toilet paper has been used as a prank multiple times over the years inside and out, but since COVID hasn't been used much.

Balloons with Bleach: Seniors returned after their last half-day of school one year to bombard the underclassmen as they left school. Balloons would have been okay but they were filled with bleach. It had caused damage to outfits and was very irritating to skin. After that year, I was stationed on the drive going to M-59 to stop seniors from coming back on campus.

Crickets: Around 3000 crickets were released all over the building. I was in the cafeteria and I swear it seemed like 2999 were released right by me. They were jumping all over the place as were most of the young ladies.

<u>Fishing Wire:</u> A window was purposely left unlatched at the high school. This allowed a late night or early morning entry for some seniors. The early morning staff was met with wire being strung for door-to-door, banister-to-banister, and window-to-window. If I remember right, it took quite a while to cut it all down. Security cameras were able to catch that group of bandits.

<u>Shaving Cream Balloons:</u> Have been used twice over my tenure. Just makes for a big mess.

<u>Water Balloons:</u> One year during passing time, the commons became a water balloon explosion. The seniors' last day was the next day so they had decided this was one of their last passing times through the commons and it was to be used for a prank location. The balloons had been hidden everywhere and when the bell sounded the balloons had gone flying.

 The cameras in the buildings these days make it difficult for senior pranks being set up to go undetected, and the same goes for those seniors who are the instigators of the pranks.

Chapter Thirty-nine

The Rap

  The end of a school year is always busy and can be mentally draining especially for some seniors. There are so many different 'end of high school events' happening in the spring for the seniors; prom, senior night, award banquets, parties, finals, exit projects, choir concerts, band concerts, graduation gowns, invitations, college visits, etc., etc., etc.

  Senior English students, some years, were required to perform a poem or a skit they wrote at an 'open mic night'. If they could talk someone else into performing their poem or acting out their skit it was allowed. I was approached by 'Samantha' and was asked if I would be her mystery performer for 'open mic night.' "What would I be doing?" I asked. 'Samantha' said, "A rap!" Nope, that is not quite my forte. "You don't want me rapping, I replied. I'm sure you can find a teacher who could pull off a rap much better than me." "The rap song is about 'Mean Scary Mary,' and I'm sure to get a great final grade if you do the rapping. "No one would expect it," she replied. For some reason I said yes, and with a big smile. 'Samantha' stated, "'Open mic night' was in three weeks." She had told me when she completed the rap; she would get it to me. "Don't tell anyone. Thanks," she said. No problem there, no one would believe I was going to rap anyway.

I didn't think much about it again until 'Samantha' approached me two and a half weeks later with the final draft. I took it home, and was already starting to panic. I can't pull this off I kept thinking. It was too late to back out now so I just decided to give it my best shot; no one would take it seriously anyway.

Performance night came quickly, and I talked my daughter Stephanie into taking me to Parker and listening to me rehearse in the car. No matter how many times I ran over 'the rap' I just seemed to laugh, me rapping, what was I thinking? We walked into the school keeping my identity a secret as much as possible. We were put in a room across the hall from the performance center called 'the box.' I was going to be the last performer of the evening, a mystery guest performer. 'Samantha' came and escorted me to the back of the room and opened the curtain. The room was packed. I was introduced as a guest performer and proceeded up through the rows of students towards the stage. Luckily it was pretty dark, and I could not see the looks on the faces in the audience. Rumblings of 'it's 'Mean Scary Mary'' could be heard as I approached the stage.

I walked onto the stage, abruptly turned to face the audience and my glasses fell to the ground. As I bent over to pick them up the audience was clapping, really I thought? I picked up my glasses and stated to the crowd, "That's not part of the act!" What a way to start I thought. Finally the laughter stopped.

The room grew quiet, and I said let's snap. The whole room went into a rhythmic snapping, and I started to rap.

"My name is Mean Mary
You better not boo
Because I have stickers
And I'll find you

I've had it up to here
with snotty nosed brats
I take their cellphones,
and I snatch their hats

They argue and cuss
I chase them to the bus
I get no respect, I have to insist
The good old days I surely do miss
Children used to respect
That's a skill they now neglect

You can call me old-fashioned
But this is my passion
Helping out the school because
skipping ain't cool
skipping ain't cool
skipping ain't cool."

As I rapped the last word, I made a drop the 'mic' motion, took a small bow and walked off the stage. I could hear clapping as I immediately went to the back of the room, grabbed Steph's arm and headed straight to the car. Steph smiled and said, "You did great Mom." "Sure," I replied. I was never so glad something was over. Rapping is not in my comfort zone and was definitely not on my bucket list.

The next day the English teacher told me that I was a hit, and quite a surprise. Students told me during the day that they really enjoyed my rap, and others asked if I would perform again. "No sir, one and done," I stated. I finally saw 'Samantha' later that day and she greeted me with a big smile. "A+, she said, thanks."

That was all I needed.

Chapter Forty

Life Outside of Work

In 2024 I will have thirty years in working for the Howell Athletic Department. Working and subbing for the security team I have twenty years as 'Mean Scary Mary'. I attended and graduated from Howell High School. I think you can honestly say I bleed green & gold. But it's my life as 'Mean Scary Mary' that seems to follow me in my everyday life.

Surprise – A Friend…

I attended Mary B's (one of my high school friends) mom's funeral to the surprise of her nieces and nephews. They asked their dad, "Why did 'Mean Scary Mary' come to Grandma's funeral?" "She's your Aunt Mary's high school friend, and used to spend a lot of nights at our house when they were growing up," he said. Really!

When my friend Karl's son was in a bad accident, I showed up in the hospital lobby. Most of the kids couldn't believe I was there, not knowing that his dad and I were good friends. Unfortunately, Karl's son didn't survive so I attended his funeral as well. The place was packed when I arrived, but I found a spot a few rows behind a bunch of his friends from high school. I could see and hear some mumbling going on, but I tried not to pay attention to it. Later on 'Jim' who was sitting just ahead of me told me one of the boys had noticed me. He told the other friends, "Hey, 'Mean Scary Mary' is sitting right behind us, we better behave."

Surprise - A Co-Worker…

I was a chairperson working at an election when I was given a list of workers for my precinct. I noticed a couple of last names as being familiar, but wasn't sure if they were related to some past students. During the day I was asked what I did, and my response was, "I work at the high school." "Oh, what do you do there?" she had asked. "I work on the security team," I said. "Are you the 'Mean Scary Mary' my kids have talked about?" she asked. My response was, "Probably, there is only one Mary on the security team." She took a picture of us and sent it to her kids with a caption, 'Look who I'm working with.' Later she showed me their response, "Tell her hi. She was never mean or scary to me."

Surprise A Distinct Voice…

I worked in a strawberry patch for years and once in a while I would have to use my loud voice. Stop throwing berries or quit jumping over the rows you're stepping on good berries. People would recognize my voice and would be surprised that 'Mean Scary Mary' was in the strawberry patch. Some parents would make comments about how they could never do my job. "I can hardly deal with two teenagers on a daily basis let alone hundreds every day," they said.

Surprise – A 'Mean Scary Mary' Reunion Story…

While attending my husband's class reunion, he dropped me off at the front door and went to park the car. Waiting by the front of the room I noticed a woman getting up from behind a table heading toward me. "Who are you?" she inquired. I didn't know if she was asking because of the reunion so I said my maiden name, "Mary Wines." She gave me a baffled look so I said, "Mary Benear."

"Oh, you're 'Mean Scary Mary' from the high school, you wrote my son up twice in his high school career," she said. I replied, "Did he deserve it?" She answered, "You were the only one to ever write him up." Again I said, "Did he deserve it?" She looked at me and said, "He loved you, and yes, he probably deserved it."

I never know where I will be when the legend of 'Mean Scary Mary' will come back to bite me, or when it will put a smile on my face.

Chris Update

A Country Boy's Will To Survive

Most of you know that this is my second published book, Yeah! My first book was written to honor my son Chris. The story was about his unbelievable courage, strength, determination, and his will to survive a life threatening situation. Writing Chris' story was very difficult, but very therapeutic. I spent a lot of time tearing up over the unbelievable pain my son went through, and smiling at the unwavering support our family received.

I'm blessed and grateful for the acceptance and support Chris' book received. I'm humbled at all of the texts and messages I was sent from family, friends, and acquaintances who read my book. Thanks to everyone who purchased and read my attempt to put Chris' journey into written word. When we celebrated Chris' 'tenth year of a miracle anniversary', and my book signing, Team Benear showed up and made it an unbelievable day for Chris and his family.

The most common question I am still asked is, "How is Chris doing?" So here is an update…

Chris has made remarkable recovery strides, for his type of injury, particularly in working on his endurance. His speech has improved tremendously since his original injury.

Chris is a lot more comfortable, after 10 years, when he is in larger social settings, but he much prefers being in smaller groups.

Chris has become increasingly more independent through the years, which is a great feeling for mom and dad. Mom will always worry about her children, especially what will happen to them when she's gone. Chris will be just fine with Team Benear in his corner.

Chris has adjusted his way of doing things to accommodate his life changes. It is remarkable how he has learned to adapt.

The Buckmaster is back. The first couple of years after his accident Chris could not hunt. When his mobility and stamina improved he purchased a crossbow which put him back in the woods. It's not ideal because Chris is limited in moving and adjusting his equipment in a hurry. The deer haven't yet learned to come in from the 'right' direction, but Chris is a very determined hunter. He is back to getting some big bucks because of his knowledge of hunting and his determination to regain skills that allow him to enjoy his hobbies.

Acknowledgments

Thanks to Amanda, Justin, Stephanie, and Alex for all you did and are doing to support your brother, Chris. Thanks to Chris. There is nothing more I can say except thanks for being you!!!

Thanks to Rachel for all your typing and getting me through my radio interviews.

Janet, thank you. Words cannot express what a gift you have been to me and my books.

Alex, Steph, and Jeff, thank you for all the work you did to get my book cover designed and done, and special thanks to Alex for your patience.

Dan Zeppa, thanks for all the help with the photos and your ideas for my cover art.

Thank you to my husband Jeff for your encouragement and confidence that I would succeed at putting my security guard stories to print, and for forty four years of loving me for who I am.